AQUAPONICS DIY

REALIZE YOUR OWN AQUAPONIC GARDENING PROJECT.

A COMPLETE BEGINNER'S GUIDE TO GROW ORGANIC HERBS, FRUITS, AND VEGETABLES.

BY

Thomas Watergreen

Table of contents

CHAPTER 14: THE INFALLIBLE GROWING METHOD 115

Introduction

Get to Understand About Aquaponics

Aquaponics is used to describe a system that combines hydroponics (which is the act of cultivating plants in the water) and aquaculture (rearing aquatic animals like fish, snails, prawns, and crayfish, usually in individual tanks) in a symbiotic environment. In a symbiotic environment, there is a union of different organisms that interact together to co-exist and ensure the survival of both.

Let's start with the plants. If you're an avid gardener, you should know and understand just how plants grow. There are several things plants need to thrive, but most importantly, they need air, light, water, and nutrients. Notice that list does not include soil. While some plants naturally grow in soil and others don't, it doesn't mean that they can't be adapted to grow in a soil-less medium instead as long as their nutrient needs are met.

Plants need water to survive as it acts as their "blood," carrying nutrients around their structure in between roots and leaves. Water is taken in both by the leaves and the roots but primarily in the roots, so it is very important to dry water soil. Traditional gardening methods combine watering with added fertilizers to help plant nutrition. The most important nutrients in the plant growth cycle are phosphorous, potassium, and nitrogen. There are about 16 other nutrients that plants need, but it's primarily these three that you'll focus on for aquaponics.

Nitrogen helps plants produce leaves, phosphorous helps with flowers and roots, and potassium acts as an immune booster. Deficiencies in any of these primary nutrients mean that plants will be sickly or may die in extreme cases.

These elements are found in regular soil gardening, created by the natural process of organic breakdown. Think of a compost pile. There are kitchen scraps, grass cuttings, sticks, etc., in there. Over time, they break down and take on a dark, creamy, mulchy texture. The original items have broken down into a much more elemental state, making the elements much more accessible to plants. Think of this as nature's way of cutting food for plants to eat. As compost, these elements become bite size for the plant. When you add compost to the soil, the plant can take these elements via its root structure.

In hydroculture, plants are grown without soil. So how can a plant get nutrients if not from the ground around it?

The simple answer is, still, through the roots.

Benefits of Aquaponics

Several reasons explain why you need to consider aquaponics beyond the simple "cool" factor. The combination of traditional aquaculture and hydroponics has a whole lot of benefits, and having one in your home isn't a bad idea.

1. It saves space

The aquaponic system encourages placing the plants closer to one another than usual, saving space.

This is because plants' roots remain in the water, which is highly nutritious for plants' growth and prevents overcrowding of the space. Compared to the other gardening methods, aquaponics is the most preferred when it comes to saving space.

2. No need for weeding

Having an Aquaponic garden at home is pretty a convenient and time-saving gardening method. Unlike the other methods, you do not have to concern yourself with weeding your garden as there is no soil to favor the growth of unwanted plants. This system is stress-free and makes growing plants like vegetables at home a delight.

3. No problems like pests

In the aquaponic system, you do not have to deal with pests and do not need to worry about pesticides. Other systems that use soil pests, considerably affect the value of the plant crop because pesticides will have to be introduced to curb the effect of pests, which in turn contaminates the plants that rely on the soil for the nutrients. Aquaponics offers a healthy system that eliminates the effects of pests and pesticides on the plants.

4. No need for watering

There is no need for the frequent watering of the plants in your garden in the aquaponic system because water is re-circulated in the system to ensure that the plants remain watered and healthy. This makes the system highly beneficial because a poor watering technique can affect plant growth. Still, in this case, it is impossible because the system takes care of watering the plants by itself.

5. Encourages speedy growth of the plants

In this system, the plants are in a constant supply of nutrients and in a favorable condition and, as a result, grow faster compared to the other systems. Lettuce, for example, will take about 2 months to grow when planted in the soil, but in an aquaponic system, it would need a month only. This makes aquaponics garden the quickest place to grow vegetables.

6. Encourages healthy eating

Raising your own food is a good decision because one cannot always trust the foods and vegetables found in the markets as a lot of them contain chemicals from artificial planting methods. It is safe to say that the food produced through aquaponics is healthy. The method eliminates the chances of artificial chemicals coming in contact with the food, which might be harmful to the body.

7. Requires less human energy

In the aquaponic garden, you do not have to worry about weeding, watering, pest control, and other planting procedures, unlike traditional gardening, which saves a lot of your energy. In traditional gardening, a lot of energy is spent tackling the menace of weeds and pests, which makes gardening a tedious task. The aquaponic garden, in contrast, requires little-to-no supervision and is a stress-free way of raising fishes and growing plants.

8. New possibilities

Makes it possible to raise fishes and grow plants together in the same system, which can serve a good source of food in the household or a source of income for aquaponic farmers.

Why do this at Home?

Besides having fresh produce from your own backyard that is better than organic, having your own aquaponics arrangement does have some perks. The one thing people hate most about soil gardening is weeding. There are generally NO weeds in an aquaponic system because weeds come from stray seeds in the soil (which you're not using). No back-breaking stooping, or hours spent tilling the soil to get rid of them. You can raise your beds to a convenient height because you're not worried about heavy soil or groundwater access.

Since your beds can literally be anywhere as long as they're connected to the fish water runoff, you can also save space. Many aquaponics grow beds are even in vertical towers, ideal for small gardens or even windowsills! Your plants are not competing for nutrients, so you can grow a lot more in a smaller area. This nutrient water also eliminates the need for watering—no more hours with the hose or hefting cans of water around.

The only problem you're likely to have is what to do with all of this fresh food! Not everyone has a family big enough to cover just how much is produced. You might even get tired of seeing fish on the menu. So what can you do with all that fresh, better than organic, produce, and fish?

Simple, sell it.

Aquaponics can be a very lucrative prospect. Since you're growing the food for your own needs anyway, you can cover your costs by simply selling off whatever you don't need. People love having local and chemical-free produce. Your friends and neighbors will be your first customers. If you plan on selling these commercially, you'll need to look into licensing and business practices. Still, on a small friendly scale, most places will overlook your neighbors buying a few fish and tomatoes here and there.

The final reason you should do this at home is for peace of mind. How often do you see food recalls or scares for bacteria or contamination? You gamble with your family's health every time you buy a product from the store, no matter whether it's organic or whether it's conventional. You just never know what has happened to it before it arrives in your hand.

Chapter 1: What Is Aquaponics?

Aquaponic gardening is a system of food production that combines aquaculture and hydroponics. Aquaculture is the process of raising aquatic animals such as fish, prawns, crayfish, or snails in tanks. Hydroponics is the process of cultivating plants in a symbiotic environment, in water.

The availability of high-quality fish has been decreasing over the last several decades. Overfishing, habitat destruction, and ecological damage have decreased the overall number of fish available for American consumption. As a result, fish farms started springing up to manage the decrease in the fish population. These fish farms became experts in aquaculture, the rearing, and cultivating aqua-life, primarily fish.

Soon, fish farms became the fastest growing food industry in the world. Aquaculture farming is much like farming used for chicken and beef; large water systems and pools are full of water and fish. Fish farms are also used for bait, growing algae, and supplying fish and plants for pet stores and aquariums. It can also increase the population of a fish that has become endangered or threatened by extinction.

The different forms of aquaculture include fish farms, mariculture, algaculture, and integrated multitrophic aquaculture; each one of these systems produces different products and provides different uses. Mariculture is the cultivation of animals or plants that require a saltwater environment. Examples of these types of products include many types of shellfish, finfish, like flounder, and sea plants, like seaweed. This type of system is set up in the ocean, where the environment is already perfect for the organisms, with large nets or tanks put in the ocean water, or in tanks outside the ocean filled with saltwater.

Fish farms are the most common form of aquaculture, and the purpose of this system is to create fish for human consumption. About half the world's fish consumption comes from fish farms; this industry has tripled in the last twenty years. The most common fish produced in fish farms are salmon, catfish, trout, cod, and tilapia. There have been several recent legislative acts created to regulate the booming industry.

Algaculture is the cultivation of algae, such as phytoplankton and seaweed. These types of products are created for fish food, feed for other animals, nutritional supplements, and for human consumption. This particular type of system is complicated to oversee, primarily the small algae, which is susceptible to small changes in the environment. Algae require specific lighting, temperature, and nutrition. There are two types of systems used to cultivate algae: open-pond systems and closed-pond systems. Open pong systems are primarily used because they are generally easy to construct, less expensive, and typically produce the most product. However, controlling for light and temperature is difficult. Closed-pond systems are similar to open pond systems, but they control both light and temperature. This type of system produces less product because it is usually smaller and more challenging to build. There are variations of different closed and open-pond systems; however, we won't cover this topic as in-depth.

Lastly, the integrated multitrophic aquaculture system is a more advanced system incorporating many different species into one system. The excrement from one species can be used as fertilizer for another species; for example, shellfish get their nutrients from shrimp and fish droppings.

It is essential to understand the necessary components, and how they work in aquaculture (or for our purposes in an aquaponic system) before starting a complex environment like this system. The purpose of this system is balanced; you are creating a symbiotic relationship where both species benefit from each other's presence.

Understanding the components of the aquaponic system will help you better understand how the system works. Now that you know a little about aquaculture allow me to give you a brief overview of hydroponics. Hydroponics is a system of growing plants without soil, in sand, gravel, and water. There are several different systems within each course; however, the most enormous difference between them is the medium used to house the plants.

Plants suspended in water without a growing medium is called "nutrient film technique." This technique was discovered by Dr. Alan Cooper in the 1960s at the Glasshouse Crops Research Institute in the U.K. This technique comprises plants suspended in plastic material. The plant roots fall into shallow water with a flowing water system flowing to each plant. Nutrients are added to the water that is then dispersed to each plant in the system. This is very popular because of its simple design and inexpensive setup. Small, and generally fast-growing, plants are best for this kind of approach.

Do not let these "simple" systems fool you; although they are simpler to set up, this does not mean they are necessarily "easy."

However, many websites tell you how to build these systems and how to set up water flow, as well as kits that include all the materials you need to start your own.

Fewer nutrients are used for this system because of the flow of water within the system and the recirculation of the water; this system also allows for effortless temperature control. Additionally, these systems do best in a greenhouse environment, getting a lot of sunlight, or in an inside room with artificial light.

From these two systems, aquaponics was born. This system was first used hundreds of thousands of years ago. There is debate about when the system was actually first used; however, evidence suggests it was used in ancient Mexico, where Aztecs used to grow plants on top of rafts in a pond or lake. These rafts comprised a series of "islands" known as "chinampas," a series of canals and rafts using mud enriched with nutrients and channels for water flow.

This was also a widespread practice for cultures in the East, where fish was a significant part of their diet. Even 2,000 years ago, fishmongers in China would sell live fish in baskets and bamboo cages. The rice paddy systems in Asia were also comprised of aquaponic elements; rice paddies floated on the surface of the lake or pond, and fish swam beneath the surface that provided nutrients. In a more advanced aquaponics system, multiple species were used to create a symbiotic relationship. Ducks were housed in cages over the fish ponds, the fish processed the duck droppings in the first pond, the fish in the lower pond lived on the waste that flowed from the first pond, which then flowed into a field with rice and vegetable crops. The water would flow from the first pond down to the crops already fertilized and full of nutrients.

As exploration and trade grew, so did this practice. Fish farming caught on faster. Soon, the fish trade became very popular, which led to one of the first times in history that people experienced overfishing consequences.

Where modern France currently is, the cultivation of oysters was expected and the production of fish for consumption in Italy. Eventually, as trade and transportation became more comfortable, the need for European aquaculture decreased.

The term "aquaponics" was coined in the 1970s. This practice became necessary because fish farmers were trying to figure out how to continue farming fish while not relying on land and water resources. A fisherman's livelihood depended on the amount of fish he could sell. As a result, a system called Recirculating Aquaculture Systems (RAS) was created. This system allowed a large amount of fish in a small space. It produced higher yields while also making a large amount of waste.

At the beginning of the 1970s, research began to study the use of plants to filter fish waste. Dr. James Rakocy, at the University of the Virgin Islands, was the primary researcher identifying how plants could be used in an aquaculture system. The 1980s marked the first invention of the closed-loop aquaponic system. Water from a fish tank was trickled into plant beds, which then trickled out to recirculate back into the fish tank.

The first commercial aquaponics system was created in the late 1980s. In the 1990s, two Missouri farmers used gravel beds irrigated by nutrient-rich water to grow herbs, vegetables, and tilapia; this was the first time gravel was used in the aquaponics arena. This system has been duplicated many times over; those same two brothers made a how-to manual that became a staple for many home-based aquaponic farms.

Research continues to study how to use this system most effectively, with the least amount of additional water and the highest production of crops and aqua life.

A recent study found that the perfect balance of fish to plants can recirculate the same water over and over within the system. If this is achieved, this system of plant and food cultivation will be the most water-efficient food production technology in the world.

There have been several recent developments all over the world, encouraging the use of aquaponic systems. In the Caribbean, a program was founded to help residents be less dependent on imported food by supporting home aquaponic farming systems. The products are then sold to tourists, creating this new economy assisting the environment and the people of the country. In Bangladesh, one of the universities has begun a program to create an aquaponic system that produces chemical-free fish and produce while making it cost-efficient at the same time.

In the United States, there's a nonprofit foundation called Growing Power, which employs students and teens to assist in producing fresh produce and food through aquaponics. They use their own compost to heat the greenhouses, allowing for the year-round production of food for the surrounding community. Whispering Roots is another nonprofit that uses aquaponics, hydroponics, and urban farming to provide economically disadvantaged populations.

This practice that finds its roots in ancient cultures continues to inspiring farmers to grow "outside the box" with eco-friendlier and autonomous systems. As the world of aquaponics grows, it is clear that the method and production will only increase in efficiency and environmentally clean practices.

Many nations are actively educating their people on the practice of aquaponics to both increase healthy, clean food supplies and decrease the need to import food.

In Barbados, in particular, they are also encouraged to sell their grown vegetables to tourists to help families increase their income levels additionally.

With more and more people desiring a more self-sustainable lifestyle and/or living off the grid, aquaponics is a popular option. It is a fair use of space and can be adjusted to individual goals and situations. It can be for the person who intends to go large scale on a commercial basis, to the person who lives in a condo, and simply wants this as both an enjoyable hobby with additional to freshly grown, organic vegetables or herbs, and fish.

There are several ways to build a system using items purchased from your local hardware store. My hope is that by gleaning information from various sources, you'll be able to fine-tune what will work best for your specific situation.

Here's an image of some lettuce roots that used a system using Styrofoam as a growing medium. As you can see, the root systems are long, well developed, and supporting healthy plants.

1.1 Creativity in Growing

If you're looking to find new ways of growing with aquaponics, then you're probably faced with a problem. While this type of gardening has its own challenges, sometimes we are faced with ones we just can't avoid. The biggest problem that most aquaponics enthusiasts face is space. You'll need enough space to deal with the tank, the grow beds (if you're using them), equipment, storage, access to water and power, and enough light for plants to grow. It is a challenging task to achieve a comfortable balance. Still, when faced with an environment that isn't conducive to growing plants successfully, sometimes you have to get creative.

- **Space**

If your first obstacle is space, then you're going to need to look at growing upwards. This means creating vertical towers or guttering arrangements that are held above your fish tank. Your fish won't be affected by lower light, and it will help you keep the algae bloom down by shading the tank. Your compromise with such a system is that you're going to be limited to the type of plants you can grow. Plants that have extensive root systems or that require extra stabilization will not work in smaller containers.

While this might seem like common sense, you can also look at different varieties as a way around the problem. For example, if you want to grow tomato plants but just can't give up space for a large grow bed, compromise with a hanging variety that can be grown in guttering instead.

You can also maximize your space by growing your plants strategically. Grow large plants at the back or center of the grow box and grow smaller plants between the others or in front. This provides the opportunity of producing more plants per box than trying to make all the same crops at the same time in each. As long as your system is flooding high enough to saturate the Grow-Bed sufficient to reach all the plants, your only limit is how they are organized and whether you have enough fish to support them.

- **Light**

If you're growing inside or trying to fit many plants together, then lighting can be a problem. To get around this, consider using reflective panels indoors to maximize your light. Reflectors work to bounce any light rays that aren't aimed at your plants back at them.

They also reflect heat, so if you're working with a system that needs heating (for example, in winter), then you won't be paying as much for heating by using reflectors. Reflectors can work outside, but because the sun's rays are so intense, they are not advised. A strong reflection can burn plants, melt plastic, and set fire to items, all of which can happen with sun rays compared to weaker artificial light.

- **Water/Nutrients**

There really isn't a compromise when it comes to the size of your pump. If there's one thing you should opt to go bigger with, it is the pump. The pump is what pushes water and nutrients around your system, and if it's not strong enough, you'll find that the plants that are further from the water input may not get watered at all, or in a grow bed environment, the water level may not reach the roots. Plants must have water and nutrients, or they will die; there is no compromise. What you can get creative with here is to have two smaller pumps as your system grows and create two smaller systems cycling off a large fish tank. This will also be a cost-effective way of increasing your system without wasting the pump equipment you already have.

Because your fish provide the nutrition, you also can't compromise on the size of your tank. Without enough fish, plants will not get the nutrients they need to thrive. Too many fish and overcrowding can cause disease, death, and fights, depending on your variety. You can, however, compromise on your type of fish. Some fish are much larger than others, and only opting for a smaller array can mean you'll be able to get more fish per tank. This will up your nutrient level in the water. The same can be said for choosing certain varieties of fish over others since they produce more significant amounts of waste.

- **Heat**

While most plants will not need extra heating in an indoor environment, if you want to grow year-round, you'll have to consider heating. Tropical fish species like Tilapia also require heating if you plan on growing year-round in a non-tropical climate. To maximize your heat, insulate the fish tank well and consider adding a reflective cover in summer and a black one in winter if you're growing outside. Black absorbs heat while the reflective surface will direct it away on hot days. You can also help maximize your heat by using reflective panels on your lighting if you're indoors. The problem with this is that it's easy to overheat your plants and your fish, so you'll also need a ventilation system.

The first thing to do when figuring out the best way to grow is to look at what problems you're facing with your space and tackle them accordingly. Let's see a few alternative ways you can set up a system to grow plants well.

Chapter 2: Why Should You Choose It?

2.1 Why Aquaponics?

The basic understanding of Organic is that the food was grown according to specific guidelines determined by the USDA that forbid the use of insecticides and requires strict adherence to the conservation of biodiversity and maintaining the welfare of animals. Essentially, this refers to the way Agriculture is raised and processed. The regulations differ significantly in every country. United States' crops labeled organic needs to be raised free of synthetic pesticides, bioengineered genes (GMO's), and petroleum-based and sewage-based fertilizers. For livestock raised for meat, eggs, or dairy products to be labeled as organic, they must have access to the outdoors for the majority of the day, daily. They must also be fed organic feed and cannot be administered any antibiotics, growth hormones, or any by-products of animals.

Additionally, if you choose to get locally grown food versus shipped organic, you are aiding the local economy. More money goes to the local farmer instead of the expense of marketing, packaging, and distribution. In the U.S. alone, food will likely travel approximately 1500 miles. To maintain freshness during the trip, the produce is picked before it is ripe. It will ripen during travels. The food is processed with preservatives or other processes to keep it from going bad before sale. This means that food purchased from local farmers will be fresh and have much more flavor.

By choosing to grow your own food at home, you are getting the benefits you would from organic and locally grown and having the added benefit of saving money.

To fully grasp how immensely beneficial Aquaponics is and why you should use it, it is essential to also know about its roots, Hydroponics and Aquaculture. By comparing the three different systems, understanding their purpose, and noting their advantages and disadvantages, you will have a much better idea of which method is best for you. I believe that, like myself, you will gain a deeper appreciation for what Aquaponics can do for you as a new home garden and fish cultivator. Through experiencing Aquaponics, you may expand further either into business endeavors or into larger home systems.

Hydroponics

Hydroponics is a soil-free system of cultivating plants. In this system, the plants sit directly in the nutrient-rich water or are placed in soil-free media such as gravel where the water can easily flow through. Once the plants use nutrients, it is necessary to add more nutrients or recycle the water.

Aquaculture

Aquaculture means water life and is, therefore, is a system of cultivating fish. This system is basically tanks or aquariums where fish can be bred and grown and requires constant filtration to maintain clean water where fish could live and thrive.

Aquaponics

Aquaponics is a system that combines Hydroponics and Aquaculture to cultivate both fish and plants together in one harmonious ecosystem. In Hydroponics, it is vital to recycle the water and add much-needed nutrients for the plants. In Aquaculture, it is critical to have water filtration for your aquatic species. By combining the two, Aquaponics removes the need for wastewater, filtrate, and fertilization. Additionally, time and energy are reduced in the process.

It may just be the perfect marriage, but as in any marriage, there is some work involved in keeping everyone happy and healthy. In the end, it is all worth it. This union has created so many positives that make the negatives insignificant. Besides, it is outweighed by the benefits.

The following chart will show the benefits and drawbacks to all three:

2.2 Compare and Contrast

Based on the chart provided, it is clear that there are pros and cons to all three. It really is up to the individual as to which system they prefer. Still, in my opinion, there is really no reason to look anywhere else but to Aquaponics for my cultivation needs.

We will clarify what has been pointed out in this chart

	NO SOIL NEEDED	CHEMICAL FERTILIZERS
	FAST GROWTH	TIME INTENSIVE
	MAKE BETTER USE OF SPACE AND LOCATION	DAILY MONITORING
	CLIMATE CONTROL REMOVING SEASONAL BARRIERS	SYSTEM FAILURE THREATS
	CONTROL OVER	EXPENSES

	WHAT PLANTS EAT	
	CONTROL OVER pH	LONG RETURN PER INVESTMENT
	NO WEEDS OR PESTS	DISEASES AND PESTS MAY SPREAD QUICKLY

2.3 Hydroponics Pros and Cons

There is no soil needed in a hydroponics system. It produces fast growth of plants while making better use of space and location. Hydroponics is climate controlled, so it removes any seasonal barriers that one would experience in a regular garden or farm. You have complete control over what your plants eat because you have to feed them nutrient concoctions or chemical fertilizers daily. You have control over pH levels. There are no weeds because of the lack of soil, and the use of insecticides removes the potential for pests.

On the flip side, chemical fertilizers may be great for your plant growth. Still, they may not necessarily be safe for human ingestion, and therefore a vigorous washing process must be undertaken. Hydroponics is time-intensive and requires daily monitoring. It is essential to conduct system checks throughout the day because a system failure can be catastrophic to your production.

Hydroponics is not easy on the wallet. It can get quite expensive to maintain, and the return on your investment may take quite a long while to occur.

As mentioned before, pesticides may be used. Still, they would defeat the purpose of a healthy product, so other measures would need to be taken to ensure pest control. If pests or diseases do show up, the spread in this type of environment can be speedy.

	SOURCE OF FOOD FOR PEOPLE AND MARINE SPECIES	WATER IS DISPOSED OF
	SOURCE OF INCOME	WASTE OF NATURAL RESOURCE
	FLEXIBILITY TO BUILD FISH FARMS, TANKS, AND CAGES ANYWHERE	WASTE OF INVALUABLE PLANT NUTRIENT SOURCE
	RECIRCULATING SYSTEMS HELP REDUCE, REUSE, AND RECYCLE WASTE	PROPAGATION OF INVASIVE SPECIES
	REDUCE STRAIN ON NATURAL POPULATIONS	THREATS TO COASTAL ECOSYSTEMS DUE TO WASTE DISPOSAL/POLLUTION

2.4 Aquaculture Pros and Cons

Aquaculture can be used as a source of food for both people and marine species. It is a source of income for many who provide fresh fish to fish markets and restaurants locally. It gives great flexibility to build fish farms, tanks, and cages anywhere. Systems created around the idea of recirculation help reduce, reuse, and recycle waste. Aquaculture has dramatically reduced the strain on natural populations. Fewer people are fishing, and more people are breeding and raising the fish.

A major problem has occurred with water waste because many still have not incorporated recirculation into their Aquaculture setups. In addition to water waste, lack of recirculation would then waste valuable natural resources found in the water that is made by fish waste and waste of invaluable plant nutrient source. Of course, there is also the argument about the propagation of invasive species and the threat to coastal ecosystems due to waste disposal and pollution. CDC states that this contaminates the water and threatens health.

An Aquaponics Garden using Deep Water Culture

	SOIL FREE	MUST GAIN KNOWLEDGE OF FISH, PLANTS, AND MICROBES
	ABUNDANT CHEMICAL FREE CROP	INITIAL EXPENSES CAN BE HIGH UNLESS YOU ARE WELL EQUIPPED TO DO IT YOURSELF

ABUNDANT FRESH FISH	ELECTRICAL OUTPUT IS HIGH UNLESS USING SOLAR POWER OR ANOTHER FORM OF
NO WASTE	NOT ALL CROPS CAN BE GROWN IN AQUAPONICS
DENSER PLANTATION/HIGHER PRODUCTION	SALTWATER FISH CANNOT BE BRED IN AQUAPONICS
STAGED PRODUCTION ALLOWS FOR YEAR-ROUND HARVEST	MUST MONITOR NITRATE AND pH LEVELS REGULARLY
BACTERIA PRESENT MAKES THESE GARDENS IMMUNE TO DISEASE AND ARE SELF HEALING	
PRODUCE FISH AND PLANTS FROM SAME WATER SOURCE	

2.5 Aquaponics Pros and Cons

By combining the positive attributes of Hydroponics and Aquaculture and removing the negative aspects of the two, Aquaponics was born. It was not merely a merger but a significant advancement into what could be possible, not just for a few but globally! It is a soil and weed-free environment that produces an abundant fresh fish harvest and an abundant lush, rapidly growing crop. There is absolutely no waste because everything is re-circulated and utilized with no need to discard the water. Instead of getting rid of water, you would occasionally add a bit of water due to evaporation. Denser plantation equates to higher production. Because you can stage your production, you can reap a bountiful harvest year-round. The bacteria found in an Aquaponics system fight disease and heal to keep a healthy ecosystem. Fish and plants are produced from the same water source. Aquaponics systems can be created in a tiny little one or two fish tank with one plant to an enormous prosperous business farming fish and vegetation. Because they can be created on any scale, and because of the simplicity in the requirements of the system, it can be located pretty much anywhere. Aquaponics gardens do not adversely affect the wildlife population. It will not be long before you can see a return on your investment.

A very important thing to consider to be successful in Aquaponics is to educate yourself about fish, plants, and microbes. Initial expenses can be high unless you are very well equipped and knowledgeable in doing it yourself. The electrical output is very high unless you can incorporate solar power or other sustainable energy sources. Though the variety and list are long and getting longer every day with new advances, not all crops can be grown in an Aquaponics system. Additionally, though technically you can cultivate any fish, it is not recommended to do saltwater as that would require a lot more work and system additions and very selective plants (minimal options) to make that function effectively. Though the maintenance is not as laborious as the other two systems that make up the core of Aquaponics, there is maintenance involved that requires regular monitoring of pH and nitrates.

Chapter 3: Difference with Hydroponics

3.1 Aquaponics vs. Hydroponics Gardening

They sound a lot alike, don't they? **Hydroponics** and Aquaponics? They are similar in one way, but vastly different where it counts. Hydroponics means, literally, grown in water. If you take the words aquaculture + hydroponics and put them together, you get aquaponics. Let's look at the two processes in more detail to see why one will be better for you over another.

Ditch the soil. Both systems offer to grow a garden without soil. This represents a considerable benefit. Soil becomes stagnant after years of cultivation, requiring a lot of fertilizer and/or rotation of crops. Merely replacing the soil during repetitive seasons of indoor growth becomes expensive.

On top of that, the soil is easily contaminated with spores or pests laying eggs, perpetuating all of the diseases from one season to the next. Growing in the soil almost requires an outdoor garden, and living in a climate zone with harsh winters means you can only grow your veggies half of the year. Both systems offer value in growing without soil.

Instead of soil, you'll grow your plants in a biosystem of specially cultured beneficial bacteria, and your very own circle of life will sustain both fish and plants. This healthy substitute for dirt is simple to produce, and you'll wonder why you never tried aquaponic gardening before.

Fertilize the water. Both systems require nutrient-based water for plant growth. Hydroponic gardening employs chemical nutrients, which represent constant overhead.

You may obtain your growing medium from any number of suppliers, but let's face it: the uncertain role of chemicals in cancer and birth defects is generating headlines around the world. In aquaponics, you may grow *organic* vegetables through natural fertilizer produced by fish swimming around the tank. *The advantage goes to aquaponics.*

Design the right space. Both systems require light and a floor strong enough to withstand some pretty hefty weight. I was clueless. I imagined a sweet little aquarium with plants above it. I was shocked to realize a twenty-gallon aquarium weighs a whopping 225 pounds. A concrete floor in the basement sounded smart, but I was hooked on the idea of cute goldfish and had a 14-ft bay window in the dining room, so the scales became my enemy.

- Figure about one inch of fish per gallon of water. If I have a fifty-gallon tank, you'll need fifty one-inch goldfish. As they grow, that number decreases.

My research suggested that I needed at least a fifty-gallon tank, so I had to adjust my weight limits to six hundred pounds. If space and weight are an issue for you, *hydroponics has the advantage in this case.*

Both systems are going to affect your utility bills. The difference between them is that in hydroponics, the water may not be recycled. In aquaponics, the water must be recycled to formulate the rich growth medium to fertilize the plants. A high water bill would make it cheaper to buy the produce at the market, making *aquaponics preferable.*

Both require a growth medium that serves as an anchor for the plants, helps regulate temperature, and provides constant nourishment.

In aquaponics, **hydroton** is a popular form made from clay. I wanted to get a product I was accustomed to using, but all of them were on the no-no list: sand, vermiculite, peat moss, wood chips, and pearlite. On the plus side, this represented a one-time purchase, and I could live with that. I see no strong value of one system over the other because both require a mix to hold the plant.

Both systems require an investment in setting up the apparatus. A hydroponic garden is cheaper to start if you employ a **wicking** or water culture system. Both need a more complicated design for some setups, and hydroponics equals the cost of aquaponics when you add a sump pump and additional piping. Aquaponics requires an investment in fish, but the price will be less than continually buying chemical fertilizers for the water. In this case, *the plus goes to aquaponics.*

However, the learning curve is definitely higher for aquaponic gardening. Because you are dealing with live organisms to create the fertilizer for your plants, it takes time and experimentation to get the right mix for ideal growth. If you require instant gratification, go with hydroponics. If you like a challenge, like to putter with details, and are willing to wait for results, go with aquaponics. For ease and learning, *the plus goes to hydroponics.*

If you've been keeping score, you already know why aquaponics is favored over hydroponics with homesteaders and survivalists, as well as a growing number of hobby gardeners.

- Aquaponics is cheaper than hydroponics since it recycles water usage.

- Aquaponics is cheaper than hydroponics since a one-time investment of fish fertilizes the plants for years, versus buying a constant supply of chemical fertilizers.

- Hydroponics is easier to learn and operate than aquaponics.

You will learn why aquaponics is the best thing since sliced bread. Just why are homesteaders and survivalists the world overhead over heels in love with aquaponic gardening?

Chapter 4: Types of Aquaponic Systems

While this is the most intensive system of growing and providing food on the planet, it does require some special knowledge. You will be meshing a hydroponic (water-based) system with an aquaculture (animal-based) system. You must choose the design that will best meet your needs. You need to know the living requirements of three different kinds of organisms: plants, fish, and bacteria. Finally, you need to build and wire a system that regulates the water for optimal growth factors. That may sound like a lot, but don't be frightened. We'll go through these issues one by one.

The popularity of aquaponic gardening is on the rise; look for online communities and support groups to offer you additional firsthand experience for your location. You are entering a worldwide phenomenon, and there is no need to reinvent the wheel. You may be able to visit several gardens, comparing and contrasting the features you like.

If you want to take a stab at aquaponic gardening, your first decision must be choosing the type of system you want to use. The most straightforward experiment would be using a sun pond where plants float on the surface with submerged roots. Of course, most of us don't have ponds and are immediately looking at a more sophisticated setup.

Every aquaponic system must include five essential elements:

- a fish tank
- a plant bed
- a means of handling solid waste
- a biofilter
- pumps for circulating and aerating water

And these are only the most basic requirements. If you're like me, you'll want a few more bells and whistles, because what's the point of putting in all the effort, only to be met with failure because you decided to go bare bones? For starters, let's look at the types of gardens and then return to these five topics with a little more basic information under our belts.

First, look at space limitations, cost, and ease of maintenance. To help you narrow down your choices, I describe the options by three classifications: growing a lettuce bowl, growing a vegetable plate, and commercial enterprises. While many a summer found me selling produce at a local farmer's market, I wasn't convinced I wanted to implement an aquaponic garden on that large scale. Still, I nevertheless wanted to look at all options, as will you.

If you are growing a *lettuce bowl*, a **nutrient film technique** (NFT) is your best option. Don't get bogged down in how to build one just yet, but you need enough details to make an informed decision. This is perfect for small plants with shallow roots. Microgreens, all types of lettuce, strawberries, and herbs fall into this category.

The NFT is excellent for a DIY kind of enterprise. Basically, you will set up your fish tank with a small sump pump running fish water through a PVC pipe with holes drilled into it, and then insert seedlings into a small net attached to each hole. The net offers your plant structure and keeps them from falling through to the bottom of the fish tank. Your plants will extend their roots toward the nutrient-laden water, absorbing nutrients, much like a paper towel absorbs moisture on a kitchen countertop. A key element is creating a system with a trickle of consistent water flow, rather than a stagnant pool of dank, smelly water. These tubes take the place of those traditional to grow trays dominating garden centers every spring.

Your NFT system can be as large or small as you want it, as sophisticated or simple as your budget demands. Large sheets of Styrofoam will work just as well as holes drilled into PVC pipes. We'll cover the actual construction, but you want to factor the essential principles into your choice of set up.

Another simple form of watering a nutrient film is an **ebb and flow** system of flooding the growing bed, then letting it drain back down into the fish tank. Your roots are saturated with the nutrient-rich water and exposed to it for a more extended period, in contrast to the dripping method of percolating your water and feeding small amounts to your plants constantly. It requires proximity several times a day or a timer to regulate consistent watering.

A vital feature of a garden fed with a nutrient film is creating a bed of growth medium in which the water is made perfect for both fish and plants. It should run through the growth media on its way up to the plants and trickle back down to the fish after the plants have done their magic.

A **deep water culture** (DWC) has been valuable throughout history. Early Aztecs (around 1000 BC) created rafts and grew plants resting on their surfaces, with roots dangling in the water. They circulated their water and waste around the rafts to fertilize their crops. Some Asian cultures used ponds and natural sources of water for growing their food, and also created floating gardens. It worked exceptionally well for growing rice.

However, you don't need to live in a pond or lake. You can accomplish the same technique with tanks to hold your water. This is perhaps the simplest and least expensive form of aquaponic gardening. Your plants may rest on the surface of the tank, roots fully submerged into the water. You still have the option of inserting canals and pumping the water through two tanks. Nevertheless, you can certainly start small and increase your level of complexity with experience.

You will obviously still need a fish tank to act as a home for your guests of honor. You may even need a **biofilter** to transform fish waste into nutrients for your plants. You will probably want a filter to remove solid waste or plant material from infiltrating or clogging your system. If you install canals, you will need a pump to force water through your system to ensure the water is recirculated. As with all fish tanks, you'll need an aerator to maintain a high level of oxygen for your environment.

This is scalable, meaning you can use either an aquarium, a stock tank, or plastic tubs. You only need to maintain the correct proportions of volume, fish, and plants to achieve the desired results. I've split up the requirements in maintaining your enterprise from the mechanics of setting it up, so your eyes don't glaze over with an information overload. I promise you: it's not hard, and you can do this. For now, just decide on how you want to grow your plants.

A **media based system** is the option of choice if you want to grow larger plants like tomatoes, zucchini, and other items for your *vegetable plate*. It will function more like your traditional backyard garden since plants will grow in small pebbles replacing soil. In an aquaponic media-based garden, you will incorporate a five-step process:

1. Choose a fish tank. You can repurpose an old bathtub in the basement with grow lights or have an aquarium next to a window, but first and foremost, you need a place for fish. The fish eat food and produce waste.

2. Most aquariums already need small pumps for aerating the water. You will also install a small sump pump to cycle water waste to your plants.

3. Your gardening container, ideally about twelve inches deep, will house the growing medium. You

will need to purchase some form of **LECA** (Large Expanded Clay Aggregate), a product akin to **hydroton** pebbles, which will provide a petri dish for culturing bacteria from your fish waste. This is where the magic happens. The bacteria convert fish waste laden with ammonia into fertilizer, a nitrate your plants will use for growth. You are creating a sustainable biofilter and your own mini **nitrogen cycle**.

4. Your plants will absorb the nitrates and, in the process, purify the water.

5. Clean water is siphoned back to the fish.

Your final consideration in designing your setup is deciding on how and where you will grow your plants. Is this going to be in the backyard? Of course, your climate and your goals dictate the answer to this question, but it bears an impact on the type of system you're creating. Will it be in a **high tunnel**? Will it be indoors with natural light? Will it rest in the basement with **grow lights**? Will you be growing plants vertically? A towering garden works incredibly well in apartments with limited space and for the artist who wants to create not just a garden, but a work of art.

These questions all figure into your choice of design and need to be weighed. Crystallize your needs and hopes, sketch out a plan.

Even though we own a high tunnel, I opted for indoor construction. In our frigid winters, the high tunnel extends the growing season, but when the first freeze hits, all plants go dormant. Only mature plants can be harvested, and then, only in the afternoon as the plants perk up and shrug off the frost. Installing an aquaponic garden in my high tunnel wouldn't provide the kind of fresh vegetables I wanted.

Since I have a dining room with lots of southern exposure and floor to ceiling windows, I opted for an indoor system without grow lights. I also wanted to keep it simple, so I decided to use hydroton pellets in small plastic pots.

If you harbor any qualms about your lighting situation, you can always find a light intensity meter and test the area you want to use for your garden. After putting a lot of time, effort, and some expense into setting up your aquaponic garden, you certainly don't want to find out you chose a dark corner where nothing will grow.

Do you see how to work through the decision making process? Take a moment right now to answer questions as your friend or partner might ask them, and come up with your own idea of where you're headed. It's that step of imagining the garden that precedes the construction and planting of any garden.

Deciding on the type of aquaponic garden you want to install isn't hard once you look at all of the options.

- A nutrient fed system is perhaps the most manageable unit to design and operate with success. It includes options of consistent watering through a drip system or periodic flooding with an ebb and flow system.

- A deep water culture requires more planning and preparation but can be very economical. Its operation requires developing a feel for the perfect watery stew, creating it by running the water through a media bed, and then letting your vegetable roots dally in the water regularly.

- A media bed requires the most considerable cost outlay and takes the most space. It closely resembles the gardens you may have grown in your backyard, the soil is replaced with the growth medium. Each vegetable is planted in a bed of pebbles.

You will learn how to construct your aquaponic garden. I'll give you all of the details required in four types of gardens. Once you have a basic idea of what is involved in each type of garden, it will be easier to choose one. Let's enter the garden gate!

Chapter 5: What Can Be Grown With the Aquaponic System?

5.1 The Plants: Deciding What to Grow and When to Grow It

I know quite several people who've just grown about everything- from potatoes through to trees. With aquaponics, you can grow almost anything, although you have to keep in mind a few things when deciding what to plant.

First of all, you want to grow plants that you will eat- I don't usually find sense when anyone grows many kales if they don't really eat them or like them. You also have to make sure that you always have plants growing in your unit- say, maybe you have only made a simple system from one IBC with one grow bed above your IBC fish tank. Ensure you don't pull out the plants all at once because you'll have nothing left to extract nutrients into the unit. Ideally, you should have a broad mix in the unit at any given instance, seedlings, half growing plants, and mature plants all at once. This way, you will be able to cycle through the plants, get rid of the mature ones, then plant another set to replace them while, of course, ensuring you leave many plants behind to use the nutrients.

Other critical factors to consider

You also have to note that different plants naturally grow under various conditions. Before you begin growing, you should start by considering the type of growing bed you're going to use. This is primarily determined by the kind of root structure plants usually have. The plants that do not have a root structure require floating beds while the root vegetables do better in wicking beds (aquaponics). Almost everything else would grow best in media beds.

For plants such as lettuce, leafy greens, or herbs, it is best to use floating 'raft' style beds. For the root vegetables, the wicking beds should be an ideal choice. If you're planning to grow tomatoes, beans, peppers, or most other kids of multiple yield plants, the media beds might be your best option.

Another important consideration is selecting the right environment in which to place your aquaponics farm. The amount of ambient temperature, sunlight, wind, and rainfall are important factors to consider to produce a healthy plant. If you choose to grow your plants outdoors, go for varieties of veggies that will grow best in your climate. Additionally, some areas will force you to use a greenhouse. Still, you don't have to worry, as you can easily have an indoor garden if you so wish.

You should try as much as possible not to fight Mother Nature even if you opt to use a greenhouse. It is usually hard to control the temperature. Plants do best when the temperature ranges are matching their regular processes. Thus, in the colder months, you should look to grow cold-weather crops; in summer, you have to grow the warm weather plants. Take a look at the following images to learn more:

Spring

NH: March, April, May   SH: September, October, November

Artichoke	Garlic	Okra	Spinach
Beans	Herbs	Onions	Squash
Cantaloupe	Kale	Parsley	Strawberries
Carrots	Kohlrabi	Parsnips	Swiss Chard
Collards	Leeks	Peanuts	Turnips
Corn	Lettuce	Potatoes	Tomatoes
Cucumber	Melons	Pumpkins	Watermelon
Eggplant	Mustard Greens	Radish	Zuccini

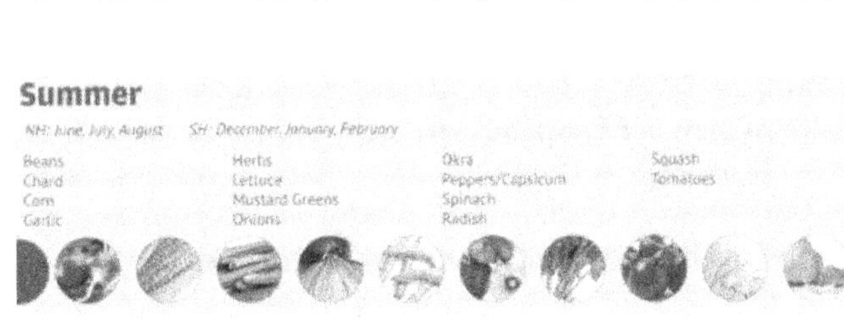

Summer

NH: June, July, August   SH: December, January, February

Beans	Herbs	Okra	Squash
Chard	Lettuce	Peppers/Capsicum	Tomatoes
Corn	Mustard Greens	Spinach	
Garlic	Onions	Radish	

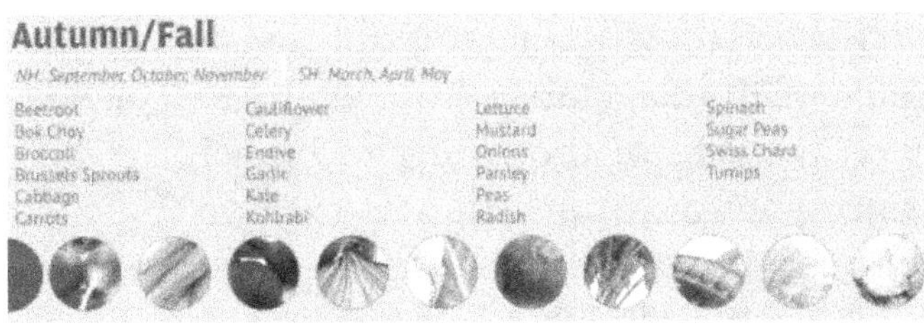

Autumn/Fall

NH: September, October, November   SH: March, April, May

Beetroot	Cauliflower	Lettuce	Spinach
Bok Choy	Celery	Mustard	Sugar Peas
Broccoli	Endive	Onions	Swiss Chard
Brussels Sprouts	Garlic	Parsley	Turnips
Cabbage	Kale	Peas	
Carrots	Kohlrabi	Radish	

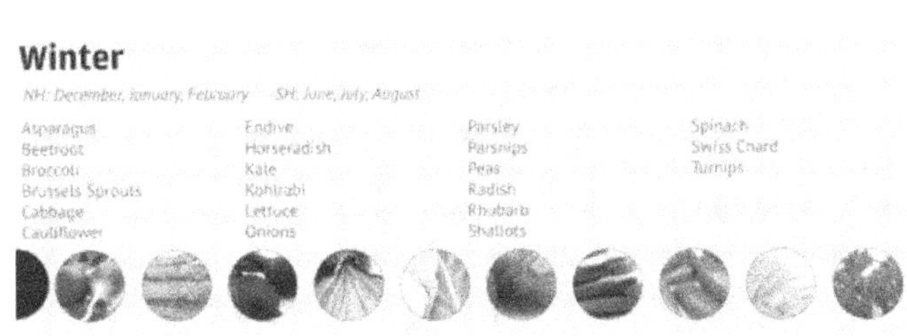

Winter

NH: December, January, February   SH: June, July, August

Asparagus	Endive	Parsley	Spinach
Beetroot	Horseradish	Parsnips	Swiss Chard
Broccoli	Kale	Peas	Turnips
Brussels Sprouts	Kohlrabi	Radish	
Cabbage	Lettuce	Rhubarb	
Cauliflower	Onions	Shallots	

Again, you have to schedule your planting times carefully. If you want to have a steady supply of food over a long period, make sure to stagger the projected harvests in a way that ensures that all your produce won't become ripe at the same time. This could easily lead to wasted product and the 'in-between' times/periods when your unit is not producing anything. If your plan is to grow multiples of one type of vegetable, try staggering the growing periods by approximately the amount of time it can take you to consume a batch.

The yield (and some of the best veggies to start with)

If your aim is to have more variety in your diet, you could also try overlapping the growing periods of three or more types of vegetables. It can take quite a while to perfect this process such that it matches your own consumption as well as the decomposition rates of the vegetables you've already picked. Making an error on the side of producing too much is really not a bad thing since you can simply donate excess veggies to friends or use the various means available to preserve them for later, such as dehydrating, freezing, or canning.

Some of the best veggies you can consider starting out with include:

Lettuce

Lettuce has been singled out by many farmers as being one of those veggies that has the quickest yield irrespective of the aquaponic system that you are using. How is that? Well, lettuce reaches peak maturity at about 28 days, and it grows in floating beds. When it comes to the minimum and maximum water temperatures, it is quite forgiving. It can survive a range of between 25 and 85 degrees Fahrenheit.

Italian style wax bean or 'pole'

If you want to grow a more nutritious vegetable in a brief period, you can consider an Italian style wax bean commonly known as 'Pole.' When all factors are constant, you can harvest this bean in about 54 days. It grows best in the media bed aquaponics unit. Its optimal temperatures are typically between 59 and 95 degrees F. If you really think about it, beans are generally an excellent investment because you can dry them and store them for extended amounts of time before consuming or selling them.

Tomatoes

Tomatoes, without a doubt, require some patience but are well worth the wait. They take about three months before reaching maturity, depending on the variety and strain. Just like beans, tomatoes grow best in the media bed aquaponic unit at an optimal temperature range of 59- 95 degrees F. If you're keen to get the highest yield from the tomato plants, you'll make sure to trim off all the shoots and leave only the main vine. This ensures the bulk of the primary nutrients of the plants are delivered to the tomatoes when they start forming.

Carrots

In around 65 days from the planting date, it is possible to hold your fresh harvest of delicious carrots. Carrots are preferable because they typically have a well-defined optimal growing temperature between 59 and 64 degrees F, even though they can grow in extreme temperatures in both directions. Media beds naturally provide the ideal growing environment for root vegetables like carrots.

With the different aquaponic systems, your capacity to grow crops is only limited by your desire to grow them.

The system will do most of the work for you in a regular in-ground growing operation, which means you can use your time to do more pressing things like creating schedules for harvests and looking for new and exciting applications for your crops. When you do everything correctly, you should be able to maintain a constantly rotating supply of pesticide-free and organic vegetables that can continue indefinitely in a well-maintained system.

Other great vegetables you should consider for your aquaponics include the following (with a little more details):

Thai Sweet Basil

This popular vegetable (especially in the Thai and southeastern side of Asia) is sweet and spicy; it's very aromatic with a sweet licorice taste. Like other basil, Thai is part of the mint family- with the oblong flower head typifying it. Since this plant is found in the Southeastern side of Asia, it is incredibly tolerant to high levels of moisture, which makes it a great contender for aquaponics.

This plant is known for a concise germination time since fresh basil seeds would sprout completely within 3-5 days, its harvest time beginning anywhere from 15- 25 days. To make the most of this advantage, just ensure you never harvest more than a quarter to a third of the plant at once; leave enough for regeneration.

This basically prevents the plant from bolting and thus prolonging your growing period. Perhaps you need to know that its flavor profile peaks when its first flowers just form. To extend your harvest, you can also cut the flowers. Besides its adaptogenic effect, the plant also contains several medicinal properties, including anti-fungal, anti-bacterial, anti-inflammatory properties.

Emily basil

Emily basil is the simple to care compact version of the classic Genovese type basil, which is generally superior for home aquaponics. This plant typically contains a shorter stem length between the leaf nodes and produces a tighter cluster of leaves, which means more harvest in a smaller space. What's more, this basil is widely regarded as a long-lasting variety when cut, making it a well-suited variety for any in the home gardener.

Emily does best in temperatures between 60 and 85 degrees and is ideal for anyone who loves Italian Basil. Just like Thai Sweet Basil, Emily basil contains a germination duration that's usually quick- ordinarily sprouting fully between 3-5 days. It's harvest time, likewise, starts anywhere between 15-25 days. You should also follow the instructions indicated under Thai Basil regarding harvesting only to a certain extent to prevent bolting and prolong the harvest.

You will get a good amount of vitamin K from Emily Basil; this element is important in the blood clotting, strengthening, and mineralization of your bones.

Arugula

This vegetable belongs to the mustard family and is yet another veggie perfectly suited for indoor aquaponics. I'm sure you've noticed how common it is indifferent salad mixes; in case you didn't know, it's excellent when sprinkled on pizza, sandwiches, and things like that. This plant does not like very high temperatures but grows well in most indoor growing conditions.

Taking care of this plant is the easy part, and it can reach sizes of 15 inches across- this means you harvest regularly! Its germination time is also relatively quick- just like most brassicas- as it sprouts within 4-7 days. If you want to use it for salad, harvest the baby leaves or wait for them to mature so that you cook and consume them large. You can also use the cut and come again to extend the harvest and harvest the outer leaves to leave the middle leaves and the fresh growth intact. This also discourages the crop from bolting.

Also, make sure you harvest the entire plant between 55 and 60 days or when the peppery flavor has become too strong for your taste – which is actually a good sign of bolting. Arugula is also very rich in potassium, vitamin C, and packed with antioxidants that support your health and general well-being.

Apart from the vegetables above, we also have:

- Pak choi

- Swiss chard

- Sint

- Chives

- Kale

- Watercress

- Most common house plants

- Plants that contain more nutritional demands and only (usually) do well in heavily stocked and well established aquaponic units such as:

- Peppers

- Beans

- Squash

- Cauliflower

- Cucumbers

- Peas

- Broccoli

- Cabbage

Although there are many other edible and ornamental plants that would work exceptionally well with aquaponics, I find the above crop's ideal, especially if you are just starting out not only because they are prolific, but also because they are easy to grow and very tasty. It doesn't matter how much you know about aquaponics; these veggies are sure to be a significant hit. So, get your seeds ready, get started…get sowing and get growing.

Next, we will discuss practical tips that will undoubtedly make your journey to becoming a successful aquaponics farmer easy.

5.2 Important Ways to Manage Your Plants

There are practices that you cannot leave out when it comes to the management of your plants so that you ensure optimal growth in your unit. These include the following:

1. Plant spacing

You can plant your seedlings using a spacing that is a bit less dense than for most vegetables in the soil because, in aquaponics, the plants should not compete for nutrients and water. Even so, your plants still require enough room to reach an optimal size and less competition for light, which can easily undermine their marketable quality and mostly favor vegetative growth instead of fruits. Additionally, you need to be careful about the shading effects of bigger or full-grown plants. This allows for temporary cropping of the species that are shade-tolerant beside the taller plants.

2. Supplementing iron

Many new units experience a deficiency of iron in the first 2 to 3 months of growth. Iron is essential during the early stages of plant growth but is not abundant in the usual fish feed. Therefore, you may have to add chelated iron (iron in powdered form that is soluble) to the unit to meet the plant requirements. It is best that you add 1-2 mg/liter for the first 3 months after starting up your unit and also when your unit has the iron deficiencies. Many agricultural suppliers have chelated iron so you can buy it from them in powdered form. You can also supplement the iron with aquaponic-safe organic fertilizers like sea-weed tea or compost because iron is abundant in the two.

3. Harvesting plants

Generally, the leafiest green vegetables should be ready in about a month or two to harvest. After three months, the unit should have a good nutrient base to start planting more giant fruiting vegetables. After the first period of three months, you can follow these guidelines to grow your plants properly:

-Stagger your planting and harvesting

You should always consider staggering the planting over time so that you prevent harvesting everything all at once. If this happens, the nutrient levels are likely to reduce just before you gather. This could bring about nutrient deficiencies for your plants and then spike right after you've harvested, which could easily stress your fish. What's more, when you stagger your planting, you enable a continual harvest practice and vegetable transplant that ensures constant uptake of nutrient and water filtration.

-The approaches to harvesting

When you're harvesting full plants from the media beds (such as lettuce), ensure you remove the whole root system. Additionally, shake the gravel stuck in between the roots and place back the gravel in the media bed.

You can also make sure the entire root system is removed in DWC pipes and NFT and place the plant roots you discarded into a compost bin to recycle the plant waste. You can easily encourage disease by leaving the leaves and roots in the system. Again, always use a sharp, clean knife to harvest vegetables. Also, make sure the aquaponic water doesn't wet the leaves so that you prevent bacterial contamination. Place the harvested plants into a clean bag and try as much as possible to wash and chill all the crops to maintain freshness.

4. Dealing with mature systems

-Stabilize the pH

You must maintain the pH somewhere between 6 and 7 so that plants have access to all the nutrients that are available in the water. You can add little amounts of buffer or base each time the pH reaches 6.0 so that you maintain optimum levels of pH. You can either correct by adding rainwater or any alkalinity-rich water if you realize the hardness level in the aquaponic system is too high to prevent the nitrifying bacteria from lowering the pH as they naturally do to optimal levels. Make sure to treat the water using acid outside of the aquaponic system and then proceed to pour water into the aquaponic system once you check the pH.

-The plant nutrition

A successful aquaponics system is a well- balanced aquaponics system. The primary guideline is the feed rate ratio, which enables you to balance the amount of fish feed to the available plant growing area, measured in grams of the daily feed per square meter of the plant's growing space. The ratio for the feed rate of the leafy vegetables is 20-50 g/m^2 per day while that for the fruiting vegetables is 50-80g/m^2 per day.

-Organic fertilizers

Even though most aquaponics doesn't use fertilizers when deficiencies occur, you have to add external nutrients but make sure they are from organic material. You can either use organic fertilizer as a diluted foliar feed for the plant leaves or just pour it into the root areas as it is.

The most recommended types, in this case, are seaweed tea and compost tea.

Deficiencies usually occur when there are too many plants for the available number of fish, or when feeding has decreased during the winter period. Before you add the fertilizers, ensure you check the pH to ensure there is no nutrient lockout.

-Pests and diseases

You also have to make sure you try to prevent pests using the techniques of integrated production and pest management such as trapping, installing physical barriers, using crop rotation, companion planting, and so on. If you find that the pests are still a problem, start using the mechanical removal techniques before thinking about sprays. Also, make sure to use aquaponic-safe remedies only- these may include biological insecticides, plant extracts or repellants, ash, soft soaps, extracts of essential oils or plant oils, external attractant plants that are treated with insecticides or chromatic/ attractant traps. Regardless of what you choose, don't let the spray get into the water.

-Follow a seasonal planting advice

Aquaponic food production, to a large extent, provides a way to extend the planting seasons- and mostly if you have housed your unit inside a greenhouse. Nonetheless, experts strongly recommend that we follow local seasonal planting advice. Plants usually grow better in the season and conditions of the environment to which they are naturally adapted.

The other important part of an aquaponic system is the fish. It might seem like the tricky part, but it really isn't- it's actually straightforward- keep reading.

Chapter 6: Common Mistakes and How to Avoid Them

6.1 Common Problems to Avoid

Establishing an aquaponics system takes time, patience, knowledge, and, most importantly, trial and error. Being aware of the most common mistakes will make it easier for you to avoid making these and build a successful system.

Pests

You may be surprised at how quickly just a few pests can destroy your hard work. That is why it is essential to be vigilant and take prompt action.

Pests are often hidden on the underside of your plants; if you don't check regularly, then you are likely to miss the start of an outbreak. It's a good idea to introduce insects that will eliminate the pest before it even occurs. Consider adding Ladybugs and Parasitic Wasps.

Fish Temperature

For a beginner system, you've probably bought hardy fish, but this doesn't mean that you can ignore the temperature or quality of the water.

It is better to test the temperature once every few days instead of forgetting about them and have your fish die. Temperature can be the most dangerous of these conditions. This is because it is very easy for the temperature of the water to rise due to sunlight or some other environmental factor, especially if you have a low volume of water. You don't want your fish container to be sitting in the sun. It's better to place it in the shade; your fish preferred this, and there will be fewer algae growth.

A low-cost technique to heat your water is to use flexible piping and run it through a pile of compost. Have you ever put your hands inside of compost? If not, you will be surprised by how much heat it generates!

An easy DIY water heater

You can go as big as you want with this. I would recommend using a valve system; this way, you can shut off the water flowing through the composting pile when the water gets too hot. Also, use a pressure release valve or leave an opening somewhere for safety reasons when you are not using it.

Fish Volume

It can be very easy to forget the parameters concerning the number of fish per volume of water and grow beds. Some fish can be stocked at higher densities because they are used to that in nature.

However, if you have too many fish, the large ones may eat the smaller ones, and the amount of waste produced may be too much for your plants to handle. This can result in you losing fish through consumption and toxic water.

If your testing results come in as having too much ammonia and you have more fish than your BSA can handle, then you need to separate the fish. Place a new fish tank next to your system and transfer some fish from your aquaponics system to the new fish tank. Don't forget to refresh the water from the new tank because there is no way all the toxic ammonia can be transferred to nitrates.

Access to the Fish

You'll notice some fish tanks are designed with the grow beds on top of the fish tanks. This can save on pipework but will not help you access your fish. The same can be said if you build the fish tank in a location that is difficult to access.

If you can't get into the fish tank, you can't check when a fish is ill, and there will be no space to do some plumbing. This can cause a severe issue if you need to act quickly and can't get into your tank. You must consider access before you start setting up your system.

Iron

This is one element that is often overlooked but is essential to the health of your plants and their ability to photosynthesis. It is advisable to purchase an iron test to check the iron levels at least once a month.

If iron levels are low (1.5 to 2ppm), then you can add some with an iron supplement (to 3ppm) that can be bought virtually anywhere. Using a fertilizer that is high in phosphorus will lead to iron deficiency. You can spot iron deficiency if the leaves are turning yellow instead of green.

A leaf turning yellow is a sign of iron deficiency

pH Issue

If your pH levels are off (6.5 to 7.5 is good), it is important to adjust them to ensure your fish and plants are comfortable. However, this is something that must be done gradually. You should not drop the pH by more than .5 per day. If you do, you're likely to put the fish into shock; that's not a good plan as shock can kill them.

In fact, algae are one of the biggest causes of pH levels rising and another issue that is often overlooked. Little algae are good, but too much needs to be removed either manually or by introducing algae eating fish.

Algae

It is worth to talk a little more about algae. In the long run, the level of algae should stabilize, but when you're first getting started, it can be a real pain.

Green algae are the most common issue in aquaponics. Too much of it is likely to make your water appear green and can even block your pipes and filters in extreme cases.

But this is only part of the problem! Algae can also accumulate in your grow beds and steal the oxygen that is vital to the success of your system.

It can also affect the pH of your system. It can cause the pH to swing in both directions, making remedial action difficult, especially if you're new to aquaponics. It is best to watch the pH for a day or two before reacting. If it's low in the morning and evening but high late morning and afternoon, you probably have an algae problem.

To control the algae, you'll need to add shade to your fish tank and exposed water. The lack of sunlight will stop the algae from reproducing. You can also catch it in your filters, but these will need checking and cleaning regularly.

The important thing if you are planning to use "grow beds" is that the top layer exposed to the sun does not get wet. This is to discourage algae from growing in your grow beds. Calculate 1 inch of dry expanded clay or river rock for the top of your grow beds.

It is also possible to add organic humic acid. It's an organic darkening agent. It will darken the water, preventing the algae from getting the light they need to grow.

Leaving the System to do its work

Once you've got the system working and the fish are doing well while the plants are growing, then you need to continue to monitor them. One of the most surprising and joint issues is when people leave their systems completely alone if everything is running correctly once the fish and the plants are happy. In theory, this is correct, but it is unlikely to be the case in practice.

An aquaponics system is a generally less work than the traditional approach to gardening and crop growing. But you still need to monitor the system and make the appropriate changes. Forget this, and your system will have a problem; faster than you think.

Adding Water

The quality of the water going into your system must be excellent. The best option is to choose rainwater or water from an already successful aquaponics system.

Failing this, you need to tap water. The pH should be between 6.5 and 7.5, and the temperature between 64 and 86 degrees (18° and 30°C) depending on the tolerance of the fish you have chosen to add to your tank.

Tap water generally has chlorine and fluoride in it. These are not good for your fish in high quantities. If you decide to fill your entire aquaponics system with tap water, in the beginning, it's better to let the water circulate and put an air stone in it for a few days before you put the fish in (if you decide to cycle with fish). This will remove (airing out) the chlorine from the water.

I can't stress this enough; always test your water for Ph, ammonia, and nitrites before putting fish in it. I've heard stories from people who didn't try their water before they put their fish in, and the results weren't positive.

Grow Media

We've already mentioned the different types of growing media. Many people are tempted to purchase a local option because it is cheaper. However, whichever option you choose, it is essential to go for one that is pH neutral and can retain water on its surface. This will ensure you have the perfect conditions for bacteria to breed and your plants to grow.

Earthquakes

Luckily this might not apply to you. If you live in an active area for earthquakes, you need to know there might be a tear forming in your piping or fish tank. In case of an earthquake, how little it can be, check for tears in your system.

Chapter 7: Environmental Impact

Aquaponics is a viable option for providing food in the modern world where land and resources are becoming increasingly scarce. This is especially true in the developed world where land is needed for residential purposes.

Alongside this, there is an increase in consumer demand for fish, which cannot be supported by traditional fish farms; unfortunately, this method of producing fish results in releasing toxic chemicals into the water at high quantities.

But that is not the only issue with traditional farming methods. You may be surprised to learn that it can take 13 gallons of water to produce one lettuce in a soil-grown environment.

By using aquaponics, the same lettuce can be produced with 1.3 gallons of water; that's just 10% of the original water input!

Also, aquaponics uses approximately ¼ of the space that traditional farming methods produce the same amount of food. The controlled environment of aquaponics can also help to ensure that crops grow faster. In fact, they can reach maturity in a little more than half the time of a traditional method (4-6 weeks in aquaponics for lettuce).

It is also essential to consider the effects of pesticides that are commonly used in traditional farming methods.

These pesticides will help the crops get rid of pests. They also soak through into the soil and eventually end up in the rivers, the water supply, and the food you are eating. These fertilizers can genetically modify, or even worse, kill other animals.

Pesticides are filtered out at a water treatment plant, but it still could end up in the groundwater.

This isn't an option when using aquaponics; any chemical pesticide would kill the fish and bacteria in the system. Not only is aquaponics a better option for the environment, but it is also an excellent system to ensure that you can't cheat. The plants are entirely organic.

The environmental benefits are clear, but this is not the only thing you need to know when choosing an aquaponics system.

You can decide to have the installation inside a greenhouse, which will protect your crops from any fertilizers and pesticides which are sprayed nearby, so the wind cannot carry them onto your plants.

It is also much easier to manage the temperature and other variables when growing in an enclosed space. It also means that you can keep growing throughout the year, no matter how the weather is outside.

It is also interesting to note that an aquaponic system can be created virtually anywhere. In effect, you can make the food where it is needed, effectively reducing the 'gas miles;' and the amount of pollution that is being put into the atmosphere.

Let's dive deeper into the technology that makes aquaponics special.

7.1 Biological Surface Area

What is BSA?

You may not have heard or thought about the importance of the biological surface area in aquaponics. Still, it is a crucial factor in the success or failure of your system.

In short, the biological surface area is the amount of surface area available for your bacteria to live on.

These bacteria are absolutely essential for converting ammonia and ammonium to nitrites and then nitrates, and, therefore, a healthy aquaponics system. The greater the surface area, the more bacteria your system can support, and consequently, the more food you can grow and fish you can stock.

Having more bacteria means less toxic ammonia and more nitrates, which will benefit plant life in your system.

So, if I have enough surface area, I'm all good?

This is not entirely true.

A small setup can beat a bigger one. Why? Because bacteria require oxygen to transform ammonia to nitrites and then to nitrates. If the big setup doesn't have any oxygen in it and the small one does, the small wins.

The point I am trying to make is that your bacteria need oxygen. Aim for at least 5ppm in your system.

- In a Grow-Bed, you create oxygen by flood and drain setups and an air stone in your fish tank.

- In NFT, you supply oxygen with air stones in your fish tank and biofilter.

- In a DWC system, you supply oxygen in your fish tank, in your biofilter, under your floating rafts, and in a degasser (if you need one).

Now you know what's important in your system. Let's talk some more about BSA.

The biological surface area (BSA) is measured by the number of square feet (ft^2) in your system that bacteria can live on. Imagine a square box that is 1 cubic foot. If you fill the box entirely with water, you will have 6 feet of BSA because there is $6ft^2$ of surface area the bacteria can live on.

We could significantly increase the BSA if we put some bio-media like rocks in the box, creating more surface area.

7.2 Calculating the BSA

For Grow-Beds:

There are two kinds of biological surfaces you can calculate.

- System BSA.

- Media BSA.

Total BSA = system BSA + media BSA

System BSA: the total surface area of your system (fish tanks, piping, floating rafts, liners, etc.)

Media BSA: the total amount of surface area of your media in your grow beds or biofilter.

System BSA

If you want, you can calculate the BSA of your whole system. It would be a waste of time when working with a small DIY grow bed system.

It will be of more practical use if you calculate the BSA of a commercial floating raft setup because it has a lot more surface area (the underside of the rafts, the pond liner, tanks, etc.).

Media BSA

Most of your BSA will come from your grow media or bio media. That is what I am going to discuss next.

To calculate the media BSA, you will need to know what your Specific Surface Area (SSA) of your media is. This is effectively the measurement in square feet of the media. The unit of SSA is square feet per cubic feet (ft^2/ft^3).

For example, take a handful of river rocks. You need to calculate the specific surface area of these rocks (SSA). To calculate this, you could measure every single piece of rock. This will give you the surface area of each individual stone.

Add all the rocks together, and you will have the total surface area of the stones in your hand.

Of course, you don't want to measure every piece of rock in your aquaponics system!

That is why there are common values. These will give you a guide for the SSA of different growing media.

For a grow bed:

- Sand – 270 ft^2/ft^3
- ¾ inch crushed granite – 45-60 ft^2/ft^3
- Expanded clay (hydroton) – 70 ft^2/ft^3
- Lava rock – 85 ft^2/ft^3
- Pea gravel – 85 ft^2/ft^3
- River rock – 20 ft^2/ft^3

Sand has an SSA of 270 ft^2/ft^3. That's perfect, isn't it?

Not really, while sand has a huge SSA, it is not good because it will retain solids passing through it, resulting in anaerobic zones in no time if done incorrectly.

However, some systems use sand as a growing medium. It is called sandponics. I will not talk about sandponics because I don't have experience with this system, and few people use it.

Pea gravel is not the best choice either. Because of its close-packed makeup, solids are bound to be trapped, at the top, making a stinky mess.

Do not use coco coir or any other organic matter as your bio media. It will decompose over time.

7.3 For DWC, NFT, and vertical towers

With the grow beds, your bacteria have enough space to create colonies because of the surface area of the hydroton or other media. With a high-density DWC or NFT system, there is no grow media for the bacteria to colonize. They can only colonize the system's total surface; that's about it.

Depending on your total BSA, you need additional filtration. This is called a biofilter.

With low-density DWC systems (0.3), you don't need one because BSA will take care of the little fish waste.

With high densities DWC systems (1.5), you will most likely need a biofilter because BSA is not enough to get rid of the toxic ammonia and nitrites.

A biofilter doesn't use hydroton or river rock. It uses special fabricated media, which is used for pond filtration. This media is more expensive than natural media like river rock. You probably need to buy it online or from a pond store.

Here are some common BSA values:

For a biofilter:

- Bio tube media – 125 ft^2/ft^3
- White Matala filter media – 171 ft^2/ft^3
- Blue Matala filter media – 124 ft^2/ft^3
- Kaldnes (K1) – 250 ft^2/ft^3

For vertical growing towers:

- Zip grow matrix media – 290 ft^2/ft^3

Remember the following formula?

```
Total BSA = System BSA + Media BSA
```

It applies to every BSA calculation. We are going to calculate the system BSA first and then the media BSA.

Before moving on to explaining biofilters, I want to give you an example setup of a small DIY non-commercial DWC system with a biofilter.

System BSA

$$2x \ (LxW) + (LxH) + (WxH)$$

The DIY non-commercial DWC system has a length of 10 feet, 5 feet wide, and 1 foot high (submersed area). It has a total growing area of 50ft² and a total surface area of 130ft².

$$2x \ (10x5) + (10x1) + (5x1) = 130ft^2$$

The root area of lettuce is 10ft²/ft² (average in a continuous production facility).

This creates a surface area for the roots:

$$10\frac{ft^2}{ft^2} \ x \ 50ft^2 = 500ft^2$$

$$130ft^2 + 500ft^2 = 630ft^2$$

Now we add the surface area and the root area together.

Using the system's BSA alone, we could stock only 12 one-pound fish.

Media BSA

I install a biofilter with the media K1 (Kaldnes). It has an SSA of 250ft²/ft³.

I opt for a moving bed biofilter and build it in a 55-gallon drum with an air stone on the bottom to provide oxygen to the bacteria.

I fill the biofilter with 3 cubic feet of the media K1. That's equal to 22.4 gallons of volume, which will perfectly fit in the 55-gallon drum.

$$3ft^3 \times 250\frac{ft^2}{ft^3} = 750ft^2$$

$$\text{Total BSA} = 630ft^2 + 750ft^2 = 1380ft^2$$

750ft² of BSA for the K1 kaldnes media.

Total BSA

To get to know the total BSA, I add the system BSA and the media BSA together.

1380ft² of total system BSA.

How many fish can I stock?

$$\text{Fish} = \frac{BSA}{50ft^2}$$

$$\frac{1380\text{ft}^2}{50\text{ft}^2} = 27 \text{ pounds of fish}$$

50ft² is a static value referring to how much surface area is needed to convert all the toxic ammonia from one pound of fish?

The optimal ratio to convert fish food to all the available nutrients is 60 to 100 grams/m² per day in high-density DWC. Now we need to calculate if this amount of fish can eat 60 – 100 grams/m²/day.

We have a growing area of 50ft². If we convert that to m², we need to divide by 10.764.

$$\frac{50\text{ft}^2}{10.764} = 4.645\text{m}^2$$

Because we will have 27 fish in the system at one pound each, we need to feed the fish the following amount:

$$4.645\text{m}^2 \times 60 \text{ grams}$$
$$= 278 \text{ grams of feed per day}$$

If we feed more:

$$4.645\text{m}^2 \times 100 \text{ grams}$$
$$= 464.5 \text{ grams of feed per day}$$

$$27 \text{ fish} \times 5 \text{ grams} = 135 \text{ grams of feed per day}$$

Tilapia eats 5 grams per day each day (average) to reach one pound in 6 months.

How much feed per square meter?

$$\frac{135\text{grams}}{4.645\text{m}^2} = 29\text{grams per m}^2\text{per day}$$

You notice that we are way lower than the recommended feeding ratio of 60-100grams/m²/day. This result will be good for low-density systems with a combination of mineralization.

$$\frac{27 \text{ pounds of fish}}{50\text{ft}^2\text{of grow area}} = 0.54$$

System density is:

These calculations can be a bit overwhelming, but I will explain them further. If you want to grow more fish and have all nutrients readily available in your system without mineralization, you need to increase the amount of feed.

You will need to increase the amount of fish in the system to put in more food. More food equals more nutrients for the plants. But more food means more waste (ammonia) that needs to be processed in the system.

If you add another two of those biological filters with K1 with a surface area of 750ft², you can increase the fish stocking density.

$$630\text{ft}^2 + 750\text{ft}^2 + 750\text{ft}^2 + 750\text{ft}^2 = 2880\text{ft}^2$$

We become a new total BSA of:

$$57.6 \times 5 \text{ grams} = 288 \text{ grams of feed per day}$$

$$\text{Fish} = \frac{\text{BSA}}{50\text{ft}^2}$$

How many fish can I stock?

$$\frac{2880\text{ft}^2}{50\text{ft}^2} = 57.6 \text{ pounds of fish}$$

If we calculate the feed required for 57.6 pounds of fish which eat an average of 5 grams a day we become:

This is in between the recommended minimum requirements for running a high-density aquaponics system.

How much feed per square meter?

$$\frac{288\text{grams}}{4.645\text{m}^2} = 62 \text{ grams per m}^2\text{per day}$$

System density is:

57.6 pounds of fish

57.6 pounds of fish x 2 = 116 gallons

How much water do you need?

Increasing and decreasing feed rate

If you are running low on nutrients, you can increase the feed while ensuring you have enough biofiltration.

If you have accumulated too much ammonia or nitrites, you need to decrease the feed or increase biofiltration.

You cannot have too much biofiltration. Having too much biofiltration or bacteria will be beneficial.

We have calculated the biological surface area for the media bed and biological filter media. But what is a biological filter?

Biological filters

Biofiltration is probably something you will have to use when you are using a high-density system. It will help remove the toxic ammonia that the fish create. If you run a low-density system, you generally don't need a biological filter.

To recap, you most likely need a biological filter to run a high-density DWC, NFT, or vertical system. If you use a grow bed, you generally don't need a biofilter unless you have too much fish for the BSA of your Grow-Bed.

The DIY biofilters are mostly made of 55-gallon plastic drums. We are going to fill them with filter media people use in koi ponds. They are more useful for standalone filters because

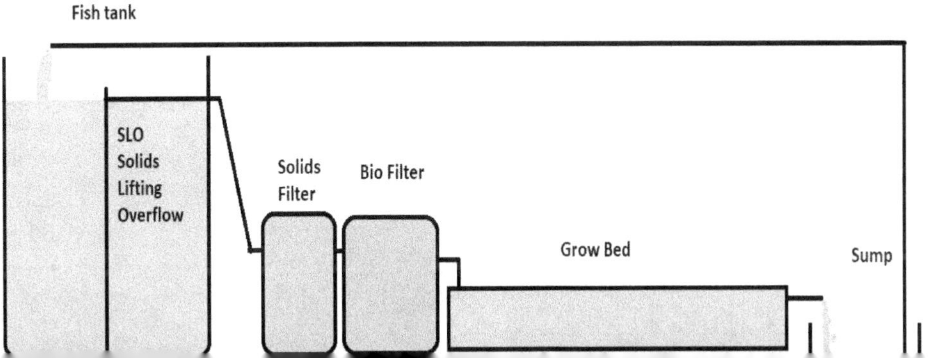

Fish tank

SLO
Solids
Lifting
Overflow

Solids
Filter

Bio Filter

Grow Bed

Sump

The water comes through the solids lifting overflow to the solids removal filter or separator. Then it enters the biofilter and then moves on to the DWC, NFT, or any other system.

Typical small DWC setup with biofilter and solids filter

There are three types of biofilters for aquaponics:

- The fixed bed filter.

- The moving bed biofilm reactor.

- The trickle filter.

It is important to note that you should not clean the media inside of your biofilter. You will remove the bacteria and basically start with a new system.

- **Fixed bed filter**

The fixed bed filter also called a static bed filter, is 'static' when the biological surface doesn't move. In other words, the biological media, where the bacteria live, just sits in a container. This can be achieved with any material that has a hi

Each color has its own density and different SSA. Don't bother with the black and green ones because the surface area is too small. Either go with the blue or the grey one.

You can lay it down in the filter, but don't forget to put an air stone at the bottom. It's best to let the water come in from the top, and the outlet should be at the bottom.

Why?

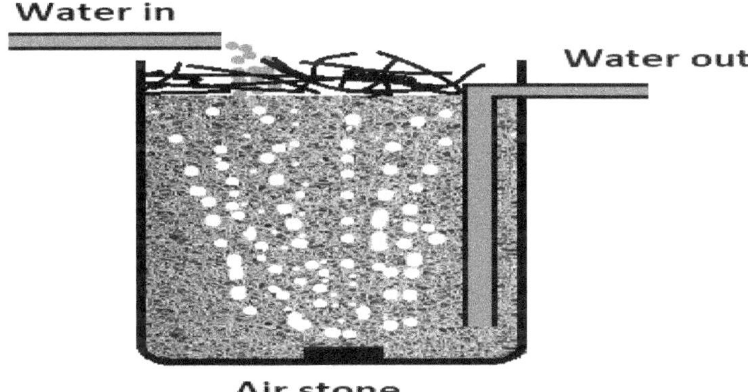

Because there may be some solids left, you could catch them by using a mesh covering the whole top of the drum. The mesh will also act as denitrification. You need to wash this mesh often to remove trapped solids.

This is an example of a fixed bed biofilter:

A fixed bed filter

- **Moving bed biofilm reactor (MBBR)**

This is my preferred type of biofilter. It is also a 55-gallon drum filled with water, and you put K1 kaldnes in it (60% filling). On the bottom, there is an air stone that 'lifts' up and circulates the small K1 bio media.

Adding 3ft³ of K1 will give you a BSA of 750ft² for one filter. Size your air pump, so it equals one liter of air pumped to one liter of bio-media.

This way, you create a moving bed of bio media. This can be beneficial because you don't have rotting solids in your filter. The movement gets rid of dead bacteria populating the bio media. Like the other filters, you can have several in a series or parallel to create the BSA you want for your system. It's best to buy bio-media in bulk from eBay or a nearby pond store.

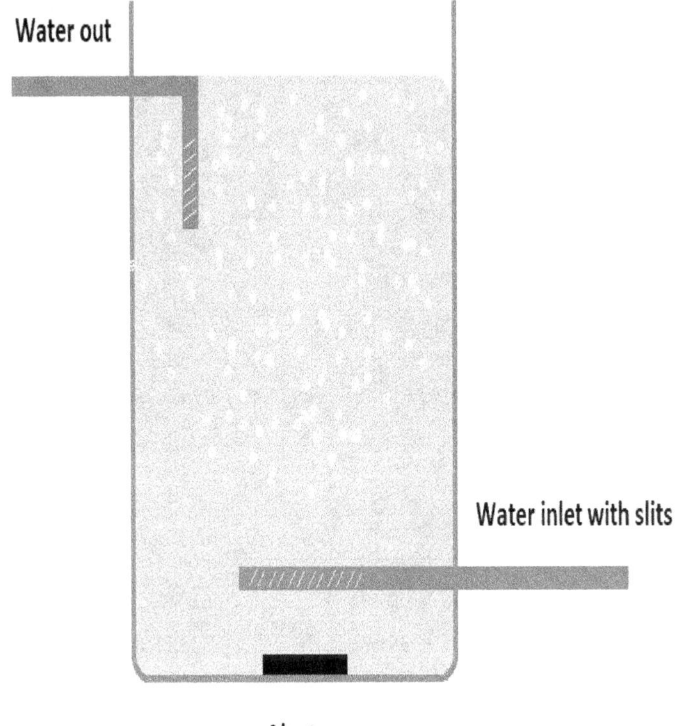

Example of K1 Bio media

A moving bed biofilter

You will need to install a little filter cap on your incoming and exiting pipes to prevent the bio media from going through your system. You can do this by having pipes with slits in them.

A look at the surface of an MBBR

Chapter 8: Possible Pests

The lack of soil in your aquaponics setup means that there is a reduced risk of parasites eating the roots of your plants. Unfortunately, this doesn't mean that no pests can attack your plants. The only way this would be possible is if you were to have a sealed room and carefully control every entry and exit point to ensure no pest could get into the space.

This will not be a viable option if your aquaponics system is outside. Even if it is inside, this will be difficult to achieve on a standard budget.

Possible Pests

Here is a list of possible pests. Afterward, I will give some tips on how to get rid of them organically.

Aphids

These tiny black or sometimes green dots can quickly suck the goodness out of any plant. They walk along the stems and literally suck the sap from the plant. This removes the nutrients and will make your plant ill; eventually, it will die.

Some of the most commonly mentioned aphids are greenfly and blackfly. They can breed incredibly quickly, it is vital to treat them as soon as you find them; you don't want these pests spreading over the rest of your crop.

An aphid (can be green or black)

Solutions to get rid of aphids are preferably organic methods.

Caterpillars

You already know what a caterpillar is. About to become a beautiful butterfly, it will chew through every green leaf it can find.

A lettuce eating caterpillar

On the plus side, these pests are relatively easy to pick off and remove; simply check the underside of your leaves where they usually hide.

Squash Bugs

Unsurprisingly these bugs are most commonly found on squash plants; they may not be an issue if you're not growing any kind of squash.

They look very similar to the stink bug, are approximately ½ inch long, and have flatbacks. The squash bug is gray and brown with orange stripes on the bottom of their abdomen.

A squash bug (courtesy of Donna Brunet)

You'll usually find them on the back-side of your leaves in a group. They can fly but generally prefer to walk on your plants. Again, these bugs will destroy the flow of nutrients to your plants.

Mealybugs

This is yet another pest that multiplies rapidly once they find a home. They tend to prefer warmer environments, so your aquaponics setup will probably be ideal! The amount of damage they do will depend on the number of pests you have; early detection is critical.

A mealybug

Mealybugs are oval insects approximately ¼ inch long and covered with white or gray wax.

Cutworms

The cutworm is the larvae of several different species of adult moths. They will generally hibernate for the winter months; unless your aquaponics system is warm enough to discourage this.

Once they finish hibernating, they will emerge and start eating the leaves of your plants. They generally feed at dusk; this is the best time to see them in action. They are effectively caterpillars but are often considered grubs. The exact size and look will depend on the species.

Tomato Hornworms

You're most at risk of getting them if you have tomatoes! They are green, generally fat, and look like caterpillars.

The adult moth lays eggs on the underside of your leaves in the late spring. These will hatch in less than a week! You'll then have larvae, which will start to eat your plants for the next 4 – 6 weeks.

A hornworm

They will generally go into a cocoon for the winter. Still, if your aquaponics system is warm enough, they may only do this for a couple of weeks. They can then transform into moths and lay more eggs to eat your plants.

What might surprise you is the hornworm; it can be as much as 5 inches long! They are pale green and have white and black markings. They also have a horn on their rear, but although this looks dangerous, they are not capable of stinging you.

You'll find dark green droppings on the top of your leaves; this will tell you the hornworm is present; just turn your leaf over to see them.

8.1 Dealing with Pests

Recognizing the pest is only the first step; you also need to get rid of the problem without damaging your system. It should go without saying that regular pesticides and other chemicals cannot be used. They may kill the pests, but they are also extremely likely to make your fish ill or perhaps even kill them. That's why you need to know the best natural methods for dealing with pests.

Having a greenhouse where soil-based plants are located is a bad idea. The pest could use the soil as a breeding ground before they move on to your aquaponics setup.

Growing your own produce from seeds will drastically eliminate the possible pests that are on a plant. The plants you buy from your local dealer could be filled with pests already.

Sap Suckers

One of the best natural remedies for sapsuckers is to spray your plats with chili or garlic spray. However, these can affect the taste of your crop and, in large quantities, can make it uncomfortable for the plants or the fish.

Moderation is the key.

Caterpillars

The simplest way of getting rid of caterpillars is to spray a substance called Bacillus thuringiensis. You should be able to get this in your local garden store.

It is a natural soil-borne bacteria that kills caterpillars and their larvae. Fortunately, it is entirely safe for your aquaponics system and your plants.

Mold & Fungus

Potassium bicarbonate is excellent at destroying virtually all molds and fungus. You can spray a little directly onto any affected plants and the ones immediately next to them.

Snails

Snails are not suitable for the system. They are in the water and can eat the roots of your plants. They also feed on the nitrifying bacteria, which will lead to high ammonia levels. Use red ear sunfish to control the snails. Preferably under the rafts in DWC (they won't eat your roots).

Red ear sunfish eats harmful snails

Slugs

You shouldn't have a problem with slugs as they should find it difficult to get into your aquaponics system. However, challenging is not the same as impossible.

Slug damage

If slugs do get into your grow beds, you can do three things:

- Flood the entire Grow-Bed to the top so the slugs in the media will drown.

- Add a small saucer filled with beer. The slugs will be attracted by the smell and will climb into the saucer. They won't make it out of the saucer and will drown.

- Handpick them of your plants and feed them to the fish.

Chapter 9: Interesting Facts about Aquaponics

An interesting fact about aquaponics is that it can be run totally off the grid. Because running your system is so energy efficient, it can very smoothly be run off of alternate energy sources, reducing your carbon footprint even further.

Think about installing your own solar panels, windmills or wind turbines, or even a form of hydroelectric power, and you are good to go.

This is excellent news for those areas that don't have access to regular electricity, or if you just want to be that eco-friendly enthusiast.

Water efficiency is a significant bonus for aquaponics; even a large-based commercial aquaponics system uses only 10% of the water that would be used for conventional farming.

Water wastage is limited as the system circulates water throughout. With limited evaporation, the only water that is lost is what is absorbed by each of the plants.

The system never needs to be flushed out like a hydroponic system. Instead, there is only limited topping up of water required to the aquarium, pond, or tank where the fish are kept.

If you are operating in a greenhouse, this is further reduced. There are even pool covers that can be added to reduce the evaporation even further.

There may be a slight loss when removing any excess solid waste. Still, it's not really worth mentioning because it's a tiny amount of water.

Year-round growing is another major benefit to aquaponics. This is especially beneficial to those out of the way places, those regions where climates aren't always suitable for growing crops throughout the year.

Think about desert climates as well as those that have shorter seasonal growing periods for certain cultivars.

Imagine being able to grow tomatoes all year round, having delicious Trout available throughout the year.

In many of these places finding fresh produce like tomatoes are almost impossible and extremely expensive.

Think of the costs involved in getting these herbs, vegetables, fruits, and fish to these out of the way places.

Through the solution of aquaponics, many, if not all, of these problems can be overcome, and fresh, healthy, organic food products can be grown, delivered, and consumed very close to the source.

9.1 Understanding Fish Diseases

Three different types of stress that your fish could be subjected to, and we are going to look at each of these here. They are:

1.   Biological Stress

2.   Chemical Stress, and

3.   Physical Stress.

Each of the above can be recognized and dealt with as follows:

Biological stress — when your fish is facing biological stress, there are various parasites, viral diseases, bacteria, or fungi in the area that are affecting them.

These unwanted organisms usually are always around but only become a problem as soon as the conditions for them to thrive are just right.

You will know that there's a problem with your fish if they begin to behave in the same way as if they were under physical stress.

This includes eating less or not eating at all. They visibly move from the state where they were thriving, and you can begin to see that there is a specific change happening.

They could also begin bumping into the walls of the aquarium, trying to escape the light because they are feeling more sensitive towards it.

Many of these symptoms will have a genuine treat for your fish.

You can sort out biological stress by adding salt to the water to help them fight off some of these unwanted diseases; however, it is important to get the ratios right because too much salt can be harmful to your plants.

It's recommended that instead of adding sodium chloride to take care of the problem, look for just chlorine (but in really low doses).

It's actually the chlorine that positively affects the fish and warding off this unwanted bacteria.

There are also some more plant-friendly solutions out there, like magnesium chloride or potassium chloride.

 These will not only benefit your fish but will keep your plants safe at the same time.

Chemical stress — is usually as a result of your water quality. If there's a problem with either ammonia or nitrites in your water, your fish are going to become stressed.

If your pH levels are low, this can also place your fish under undue pressure. Remember that your nitrate levels can go up to 500-700ppm quite safely without disrupting any of your fish.

Remember to remove any unconsumed food from the tank or pond within 30minutes of feeding (every feed).

If your filter it is not working sufficiently to remove unwanted waste from the tank or pond, chemical stress is very likely.

All this unwanted waste in the tank reduces the amount of dissolved oxygen (DO) in the water, and your fish will soon start being oxygen-deprived.

Physical Stress — is probably the most common type of stress that your fish could ever go through because there are so many external and internal factors that could apply towards the creation of physical stress.

Some of these include water temperature. Fish do not have the means to self-regulate their internal body temperature because they are cold-blooded animals.

We need to know the temperature range that our fish will thrive in and maintain the water temperature within those ranges to prevent them from going into shock.

Symptoms of temperature problems are very similar to those of when they are suffering from biological stress – they either stop eating altogether, or the amount of food they consume will be reduced.

We need to watch for optimal thriving temperatures with our fish because they can also become more susceptible to diseases that are always present.

Many other things physically stress fish out; these are things like a sudden change in light (when we turn lights on and off, the fish become confused — we are telling them that it is now daytime).

If they are confused, they will start swimming into the sides of the tank. Loud noises and tapping against the tank are also a problem for your fish.

Because they hear throughout their bodies via vibrations, something as simple as tapping against the tank can sound like screaming for them. This will set them into a state of stress.

Finally, most fish prefer to live in calm waters. Examples of these would be Perch and Tilapia.

Other fish prefer to have a form of a currently available in their tank – think of any typical river fish such as Trout.

We need to think about all of these things and monitor any undue stress that we may be causing our fish.

Chapter 10: Best Fish for Aquaponics

Yes, you are supposed to keep fish, but not just any kind of fish. It all depends on the purpose of your garden. Are you rearing fish for human consumption? Or do you just need the fish to grow the plants? There are many different reasons for breeding fish. Here is a list of fish that are best suited for an aquaponics system:

1. Tilapia

It is a common fish in many aquaponics gardens. Many farmers prefer it because it is bred easily, and hardy — tilapia can withstand extreme weather — and take little time to mature. Tilapia is also edible and quite a delicacy. Many farmers keep them for this particular reason.

Tilapia is found mainly in rivers, lakes, ponds, and other shallow water bodies. There are many — about a hundred — species of the fish. Tilapia is appropriate for the aquaponics system as its leading food is plants, with algae being a favorite. The fact that they can correlate with plant life makes them suitable for aquaponics. The ideal environment for them in an aquaponics garden is being kept in warm water.

2. Trout

This kind of fish is excellent for lower temperatures of about 10°C to 20°C. Its palatability makes it a preferred choice for many farmers. It also matures quickly, so it can be farmed after a short period. Unlike their counterparts, tilapia, whose diet is plant-based, trout are carnivorous. Their primary food is small fish and other small water animals such as worms and some flies. Trout are versatile when it comes to habitat as they can live in different habitats. They can camouflage themselves and, therefore, easily blend into different environments. Farmers also like them for their impressive food conversion ratios.

3. Goldfish

These are probably the most commonly domesticated fish. Their domestication can be traced down to several decades back. You may have spotted them in aquariums in homes and museums. These fish are not edible but are usually used for decorative purposes. They are small in size and brightly colored.

Goldfish are naturally omnivorous; they can eat small animals such as insects and feed on various plants. You will usually find them where there is plant cover as they breed under this cover. Therefore, the fish tank they are kept should have several plants to allow for breeding and double as food. When they feed, they release a lot of waste that is used for fertilizing the crops

4. Carps

These fish exist in different species, and their natural habitat is freshwater. They are, however, versatile: they adapt easily to different habitats. Carps are a famous choice by many farmers because they are edible. They are extensively used for food, recreation, and aquaponics. Domesticating them is relatively easy too.

Carps feed on plants and small and soft-bodied water animals. They reproduce in reasonably large numbers and populate quickly.

5. Catfish

They are one of the most common fish in aquariums. Catfish, unlike many other species of fish, has no scales and is sensitive. When keeping it in a fish tank, it has to be skinned. They exist in almost every part of the world except the icy areas of the North. You can identify it from its ray-finned fish and whiskers on its anterior parts.

Catfish have speedy growth. They can grow to huge sizes when well fed. They are edible and are a widespread target for anglers. They thrive in warm climates as it provides optimal conditions for their reproduction and survival.

Catfish are omnivorous; they feed on smaller fish, insects, aquatic invertebrates, and plants. There are several species of catfish, with the blue catfish and channel catfish being the most commonly consumed species. It is preferred as a food fish because it is rich in vitamin D. Farmers love catfish because of its good food conversion ratio.

6. Koi

You may have come across these conspicuous fish as an embellishment in homes and various other places. The fish are alluring owing to their flashy colors. They occur in different sizes and colors and have therefore been a favorite for decoration purposes.

Koi survive and thrive in aquaponics, making them a top choice for farmers. Another merit is that they live longer. Therefore, you will not need to continually acquire new fish every now and then. Koi are hardy and resistant to relatively harsh weather and disease-causing parasites.

Just like most beautiful fish, Koi are not eaten. They are used primarily for decoration. They feed on the vegetables and other smaller fish. Koi need a little extra care: their fish tanks have to be rid of gasses and oxygen supplied to them, especially in small tanks and cold winters. Koi are covered in large scales that will need to be removed. These fish are more expensive than most other types (beautiful things don't come cheap).

7. Largemouth Bass

This freshwater fish is olive-green in color and thrives in low temperatures. It is carnivorous—its diet consists of small fish, shrimps, insects and scuds, snails, snakes, little birds, and other small animals. The largemouth bass is a member of the sunfish family. It is convenient for the aquaponics system as it can feed on a variety of foods.

The largemouth bass is edible, and many consumers love it because of its strong taste. The smaller version of the fish tastes better than the grown adults, mostly because of its diet. The taste of largemouth bass is unique, and you would easily recognize it if you ate fish often.

Whatever the purpose, it is crucial that you take absolutely good care of the fish. Some fish are quite sensitive, and neglecting their maintenance may lead to the loss of both fish and time. In the entire system, the fish play the most crucial role.

When choosing the fish for your system, decide whether you prefer fingerlings or fry. This may be mostly dependent on your budget. The fish fry will cost you less, whereas fingerlings will cost more. However, fish fry takes a long to grow and may not benefit you until it is well mature. Fingerlings mature faster and release substantial waste even in their early stages. If you have a need to reap quickly from your aquaponics garden, you could acquire already mature fish, which will, in turn, cost you more.

Chapter 11: Understanding the Nutrient Cycle

11.1 Nutrient Cycle & Bacteria

Well, if you thought your science lesson was over, you were definitely mistaken. Chemistry 101 continues as we delve deeper into Aquaponics. It is time to learn about a major part of the circle of life in our Aquaponics system. Many seem to forget about this process and how it works to simply define how exactly Aquaponics works. I imagine the same is true for how cow manure fertilizes the crops. How many people have actually thought about how and why manure actually helps the crops grow? I know I never gave it a second thought. I just knew it worked. Well, in Aquaponics, it is extremely important to know how to fish poop feeds your plants. Because we are essentially creating an ecosystem, for the ecosystem to function like a natural ecosystem, we have to help it out and play "mother nature" in our garden. How can we help our fish to help our plants to help our fish? Well, Mother Nature does her job so efficiently that we don't think a lot about the inner workings and intricacies behind nature and how it can thrive.

Ammonia, Nitrites, and Nitrates

Nitrogen is extremely important to plants; although nitrogen is found in the air we breathe, it is not in a form that is usable to plants. Hence, plants need to get their necessary nitrogen from an alternate source. Using an Aquaponics system, plants can get nitrogen in the form that's suitable to them.

This form of nitrogen is called Nitrate, and it is made by bacteria that process Ammonia to grow.

These bacteria are known as beneficial bacteria because they help achieve a positive outcome. Penicillin falls in this category. The more beneficial bacteria there are, the better it will be for your ecosystem because of the fish release ammonia constantly through their waste and through their gills. The bacteria eat the fish waste and process it, turning ammonia into nitrates for the plants to get fertilized.

When you first start your Aquaponics system, there are specific stages you take in which plants and fish are introduced. Before both, you will simply have water that will not only be used to test and make sure the system flows properly, but also to test for temperatures, oxygen, pH, and other balances. One of these tests you will run periodically is to test for ammonia, nitrites, and nitrates. Obviously, we can't see bacteria because they are microscopic, so this test is very important. You might be thinking at this point:

- How can we be testing for something that comes out of fish when there are no fish?

- How can we introduce plants before fish when fish feed the plants?

Both are good questions. Water in the tank right now will show no ammonia, no nitrites, and no nitrates, which as the question above pointed out, is a problem for the plants. It is not only a problem for the plants but also for the good bacteria we want to grow in our tank. If there is no ammonia, there will be no bacteria. As I said, this is a circle of life, and we play Mother Nature, so we must intervene and add ammonia so that there is a food source for bacteria. We essentially step in as substitutes for the fish until they can assume the role regularly.

We must monitor the process regularly, and once we get to a level that works for our plants, then we can introduce them to the system. In the meantime, as we add ammonia, bacteria appear and start to do their job of converting it to nitrate. Our measurements will gradually show a decline in ammonia and a rise in nitrites. This is the level between ammonia and nitrates. Bacteria are doing its thing, but we are not quite there yet. Next, measurements will show a decrease further in ammonia, a decrease in nitrate, and now an increase in nitrate. Soon our measurements will reflect the necessary nitrate levels to effectively fertilize our plants, which means that bacteria levels are growing. This is good news and should only take about two weeks to achieve. This bacterial process is known as cycling. You know that your garden is fully cycled when there is a continual process of transforming ammonia into nitrite into nitrate. The addition of fish should maintain a fully cycled system.

Let us go back to the question about fish being introduced after plants. You could technically add plants and fish simultaneously as long as the ammonia levels have officially dropped to zero. Ammonia is poisonous to fish, and though they produce it, they cannot live in it. Fish in an aquarium would have a filter to remove waste products to keep levels safe. Still, in Aquaponics, we need to rely on the bacteria and the plants to keep the water safe for the fish.

Ammonia kits will advise proper levels and amount to add to your tank to ignite bacteria production and eventually nitrate. As each level is achieved through the cycle, less ammonia should be added. Generally, liquid ammonia is used and administered with a dropper. Another way to increase ammonia levels is to drop a few dead fish in the water since decomposing organisms release ammonia.

The intermediary level of the cycle, nitrite, usually occurs in the second week of the process. Though it is not quite as lethal as ammonia, it is important to continue measuring these levels until you reach the third level, nitrate, beneficial to plants and safe for fish. During this nitrite cycle, do not add fish because nitrites stop blood from oxygen absorption and cause gastrointestinal, renal, and nervous system failures. Because oxygen absorption is prevented, fish can stop breathing regardless of the oxygen supply available in their water.

Plants and fish will both benefit from the nitrate level of the cycle. Once your plants are consuming the nitrates, and you are in full cycle, your measurements may reflect zero on all three levels of the cycle once again: ammonia, nitrite, and nitrate.

Mineralization

The process by which chemical compounds are broken down in organic matter for plants is known as mineralization. The media surfaces of your garden are highly conducive to this process since the water and waste from the tank flow through their regularly, allowing for the transformation into minerals and nutrients to occur naturally.

Other Additives

Ammonia is added to achieve cycling, but there are other things you could add to help your plants flourish. Adding chelated iron powder will help the plants convert light to energy and look vibrant and full. Another additive would be kelp or seaweed because they have a host of vitamins and minerals needed by plants.

Chapter 12: System Design

Before you get excited about choosing fish or plants, you have to do a lot of designing to ensure that your system will work. As you can tell, no matter what method you use to get the nutrient water to your plants, there is a fine line between too little water and too much. There are several elements to keep in mind when designing each aspect of your system – cost, location, suitability. Not all fish are legal in every country, just as some grow mediums will float in a flooding design. You'll need to do a lot of research into each before making your final selection, or you could potentially waste a lot of money.

Location

Plants need more than just water and nutrients to grow. They also need a good source of light. Depending on your chosen variety, you'll need between six to eighteen hours of sunlight each day. A south wall, a greenhouse, or artificial lighting indoors are all potential ways to get this. Depending on how elaborate you decide to grow, you can use any small or large space you have available as long as you tailor it to the lighting. You'll also obviously want to have a location with a water source, and potentially electricity if you don't want the added expense of solar panels to power your pumps.

The first thing about choosing a location is space – how big or small you want to go. If you want multiple crops or multiple fish, you're going to need a lot more space. Don't forget you can grow vertically too; we'll look into grow towers and vertical growing shortly.

While you may have a south-facing wall ideally, it may be nowhere near your water source and require extra hoses or pumps or adding in piping from your mains, which is costly. Similarly, you may have a greenhouse, but you would like to grow tomatoes or other larger plants, and there isn't enough room for those and the fish tank.

Don't forget that you also need access to electricity, which will need to be grounded away from your water source to avoid the risk of electric shock. Water and electricity are a dangerous mix, so you should be absolutely certain everything is separate before powering on. If you don't want unsightly power cords running across the house, or you're worried they might be a tripping hazard, you'll need to wire in a specific breaker and power connection for your system wherever you decide to grow.

Deciding on the location is by far the hardest part. Once you know where you want to put everything, you can start setting up.

But what if you just don't have space?

Many people worry that they need enough space to account for the grow bed and tank. Most of this is centered around thinking horizontally rather than vertically. Many successful aquaponic solutions are grown vertically. Take, for example, the popular strawberry tower. Using little more than a large PVC pipe, cap, and guttering, you can grow multiple pipes full of strawberries suspended above the ground. This frees up your ground space for other grow beds or to put your fish tank in. The same goes for using a simple wall-mounted guttering system. As long as your pump is designed to handle the amount of water and distance, you need to give all your plants adequate access to the nutrient water your system will work.

Remember, when designing your system that you want a closed loop. There should be nowhere for your water to run-off or overflow without reason. The perfect example of this being forgotten is those strawberry towers. If you measure your water right, it will trickle down inside the tower with no mess and no overflow. If you're wrong, the water will overflow out of the strawberry holes and drip down the outside of the pipe onto the ground. If you didn't buy an adjustable pump, simply placing a line of guttering under the pump or another grow bed to catch the overflow and return it to the system is a functional way of correcting this.

12.1 Hardware

Your hardware will vary depending on what system you choose, but one of the main components is what are you going to grow your plants in? If you're going with media-based, then you'll need to look at coir, rock wool, perlite, LECA, or alternatives. Don't forget that not all hydroponic media is suitable for fish. Lava rocks, for example, will raise the pH of the water and can kill fish because of that. Your first priority is your grow bed.

Grow Bed

Many people use simple plastic grow trays as these are easy to drill into and attach pipes and pumps. Obviously, they need to be waterproof, so wooden boxes can be used as long as they are lined with plastic or the wood will rot. You want to have a grow box that is sterile, meaning the medium will not in any way interact with the plants or nutrient water. A simple plastic tote from the hardware store will work equally well if you're on a tight budget.

The only issue you need to keep in mind is whether or not the media will be too deep or not deep enough to correctly grow your plants.

You want about a 1:1 ratio to your fish tank volume and a fairly flat shape that isn't too deep, so your plants get adequate light and space. 30Cm deep is about the most common size.

You also need to keep in mind that plants, fish, and hardware are quite heavy, so your box needs to be sturdy. Look for non-toxic or food-safe if possible. Metals and concretes are not suitable because they will degrade over time and can leach into the water. The same is true of some kinds of plastics, so a food grade is a good option.

One of the most common options for larger systems is IBC containers. Intermediate Bulk Containers are commercial tanks used for storing liquids or foods and can be cut or customized to fit your needs. These are not particularly cheap or attractive, but they are sturdy and come in various shapes.

Media

If you've chosen a media-based system, you'll want to decide on this next. If you're skipping media based in favor of a raft or basket, you can use the same concept as choosing a grow bed box, simply apply it on a smaller scale to how deep the roots of your chosen plant are rather than the depth of the tub. For example, a 30cm depth Grow-Bed can also be translated into a 30cm basket for larger plants or relatively smaller for anything less.

When choosing to grow media, there are several options available. You'll want to choose something that is inert and doesn't affect the water for the fish.

Rockwool is iffy because of this as small microscopic pieces can detach and end up being consumed by the fish, so most aquaponic growers choose sturdier alternatives like coir, LECA, hydroton, or just natural clay.

The media needs to be slightly porous so that it holds enough water to keep the plant roots moist once the water has receded but not soaked so that they rot. It also needs to have enough aeration that air can flow in and around it, so it doesn't cause mildew or mold and allows the roots access to air. Another consideration is the size of the media. This is a very small and light media that floats easily. Though it is ideal in every other way, it isn't suitable for most systems.

Coir or coco-croutons/chips are made from chunks of coconut husk. These are organic in nature and will eventually break down and need to be replaced. They hold water extremely well, and roots can easily penetrate through the fibers if the plant outgrows the space. The problem is that they also rot, which introduces the potential of bacteria or mold, which may affect fish; you'll also have to deal with how heavy the soaked coir becomes.

Expanded clay is another popular choice because it is so light that it is one of the best aerators. The balls are between 8-16mm in size and are good for encouraging fast root growth. They are also neutral and lightweight, but the real benefit is that they can be sanitized and used again. Once you have used coir, it cannot be reused, so this is a major bonus and much cost saving. These are similar in feel and use to LECA or hydroton.

Hydroton is actually just another form of expanded clay, but it's cheaper than the other version. It has a good capillary structure, which also provides good aeration and has other benefits, such as being pH neutral.

Make sure whichever medium you look for is pre-washed or make sure you wash it before putting it into your system. This will help dust or any contaminants on the media to be rinsed off before introducing them.

Pump

Depending on your arrangement, you may need a larger or smaller pump, as well as a filter. Your pump size is dependent on your tank size as you want it to be able to comfortably transfer as much water as your system needs, or you'll need to add more than one. Most pumps are not that expensive, and you'll be looking at a range of between 120-1000 GPH for most aquaponics systems.

What you need to look for is the recommended gallon tank size and relate this to the size of your tank and grow bed. For example, if you're using the simple desktop 20-gallon tank, you'll only need a 120GPH pump. Similarly, if your tank is 100 Gallons or more, you'll want a 1000GPH pump. This is just the start. It's a good idea to also look for whether or not the pump has its own filter. If you're not planning on adding a filtration system to your design, you need this to keep out any solid waste that may get in from plants or fish. A filter is a must, and having it easy to remove without tools is a big bonus.

Another important factor in choosing a pump is whether you want an adjustable flow rate. This isn't a necessity, but it can help if you have an outdoor system to increase flow on hot days and decrease on cold when plants need less water.

One of the main things to look at is that your pump is suitable for fish. Just buying a commercial water pump isn't going to work unless you're running it externally (which will require extra piping and cost). Fish tank suitable pumps use no oil and have no exposed copper. The steel, ceramic, or plastic in the propeller creates very little interaction with the water, so it doesn't become contaminated or affect pH.

It is rather unavoidable all pumps will make noise. If you're putting your system downstairs or close to your house, you'll need to keep this in mind, especially if the noise bothers you.

Some pumps are quieter than others, and while it's unlikely that you'll find a decibel rating on the side, you may want to hear it run first before deciding if you think it will be an issue.

These are really the main "ingredients" to any successful system. Your fish will need something similar to the Grow-Bed, so it's a simple matter of just buying two of them for most start-up systems. IBCs are also a good choice if you want a large tank for fish.

Chapter 13: Advanced Techniques

13.1 Advanced Techniques – How to Level Up Your System

13.2 Thinking of Going Commercial?

So you have successfully set up and got the hang of a smaller system that can sustain your family with regular seasonal crops and fish.

Where do you go from here? The natural progression is being able to share this with others.

Due to the current crisis when it comes to sustainable agriculture, insufficient land availability, high costs of conventional farming, high costs of labor, seeds, climate change, drought, and an entire host of other challenges that threaten agriculture as we know it, aquaponics can genuinely provide an answer. Let's take a brief look at each of these challenges.

Firstly, climate change has brought about irregular seasonal changes all over the world.

The change in weather patterns is apparent and is felt globally.

Areas used to seasonal rainfall are now experiencing crippling drought conditions that are literally bringing the conventional crop farmer to their knees.

They are unsure whether or not to plant their crops because rain is not guaranteed, and even a few weeks out can make all the difference for any cultivar.

Aquaponics addresses this issue because there is very little water used other than in the aquarium or pond where the fish are kept.

The plants are grown in a closed recirculating system, preventing water loss. Therefore the only water that is used throughout the entire process is either via evaporation or plant uptake. You don't even need to drain and replace water like you would in a hydroponics environment.

This system can be designed to fit into any space, making it convenient to meet your specific requirements.

If you live in a small apartment building, you may only have the space available on a countertop for a small aquarium with ornamental fish, with the grow beds above.

Alternatively, you may live on a larger property where you have access to a greenhouse. You are looking at upscaling your operation to become a commercial one.

You will have noticed that in one of the previous diagrams of a system that the troughs are stacked or separated above one another.

This saves space while allowing you maximum yield for your plants. You can adopt similar systems in a greenhouse environment, interconnecting the closed-circuit pipes, or adding raft systems that cover the space that you have at your disposal.

Aquaponics is sustainable because, with a little training, anyone can do it. The most challenging part of setting up an aquaponics system is the cycling process.

Once you have managed to get this right, and under your belt, there is very little work that needs to be done.

Most of this work involves monitoring your pH, water and air temperature, your fish, and your plants. Pretty simple stuff when you compare it to the complexities involved in conventional agriculture and the amount of labor involved. It's no wonder that many countries are beginning to teach communities how to design, build, and manage their own aquaponic systems as a means of the sustainable food supply.

Communities that don't have access to regular water or power can adopt this method of supplying themselves with organically grown fruits, vegetables, herbs, and protein in the form of fish. A reasonably small area would be able to produce enough produce to feed a community.

Conventional farming costs are extremely high when you think about all the equipment you need to invest in plow the land, plant seeds, irrigate the land sufficiently, and then harvest the crop once it has grown. It's not just the equipment cost that you need to take into consideration but also the cost of fuel and labor (even seasonal labor when necessary).

All of these costs add up—compared with a smaller aquaponics system, this can be run at a fraction of the cost. Once it is up and running, the operating costs are reduced.

The cost of seeds, pesticides, and other chemicals required in conventional farming is exorbitantly high. In aquaponics, there are no pesticides and chemicals used whatsoever.

The only costs that you would be faced with would be your seeds, seedlings, and your fish, once you have designed and set up your system.

For environments that face extreme weather conditions such as drought, deserts, or land that has eroded and is non-arable, aquaponics can be a cost-effective solution.

There have even been instances of large aquaponics facilities being set up in the middle of the desert to support the surrounding environment.

Additional benefits to upscaling to commercial aquaponics would be that food could be grown close to the source of consumption.

This would save time, energy, and money on refrigeration, transportation, and chemicals currently being used on the foods that we are currently purchasing from your local grocer.

By growing close to the source of consumption, you are genuinely producing vegetables, fruit, herbs, and protein that is truly organic.

There have been absolutely no chemicals or additives included as part of the entire growth cycle.

Chapter 14: The Infallible Growing Method

I bet you read that and thought you were going to hear a miraculous solution to your woes. Every aquaponic situation is different, and what works for one gardener may not work for another. There are three main types of the system alone, so how could you possibly have a one size fits all method?

The best advice I ever saw was from Meg Stout, a leading enthusiast and aquaponics expert. She created the acronym SWANS to determine the 5 components and the aquaponics system needs to be successful.

14.1 S is for Sun

Sun or lighting is essential for plant life. Without light, your plants can't grow and certainly won't be successful. Without adequate light, they will fail to flourish. We've looked at lighting much more in-depth so far, and if you're serious about your success, you'll want a light meter to determine that your plants are getting the right amount of light. It's practically impossible with consumer-grade equipment to determine that they're getting the right wavelengths. Still, if you want to splurge for those LED lights with varying wavelengths, you can play around a little bit to create a light recipe that works best. This is where your experimentation can either give you great success or cost you money.

14.2 W is for Water

Water is the very basis of your aquaponics system. Without it, your nutrients can't get to the plants, you can't grow fish, and the whole thing falls apart. Your water needs to be of reasonable quality, without contaminants, and as free from algae as possible. Water affects plants and fish, so you've got to cover the oxygen needs for both as well.

Oxygenation is rarely an issue in smaller systems, but the larger you go, the more likely you'll need to create excess surface area for your plants and fish, or they'll suffocate.

Water can only have so many molecules of gas dissolved it in at a time before it reaches saturation and while infusing it with pure oxygen is expensive and unnecessary, having air that is too rich in carbon dioxide being pumped through can have negative effects on oxygen levels. Consider pumping your air from outside the grow room instead as a simple way to boost water oxygenation levels.

It's a common misconception in aquaponics that your plants and fish don't need extra oxygen, and you should be wary of any that advocate this belief.

14.3 A is for Air

While air pollution and breathing is something we attribute to humans having enough breathing space is part of the plant life cycle. Plants need to absorb gases through their leaves, and without having adequate space for their leaves to contact the air, they won't be able to do so efficiently. You'll need adequate space for your plants to grow and expand as well as creating enough roots.

Not every system is suitable for all plants. The root system of your plants is especially important with aquaponics. Of the three main designs, only certain plants will work with some of them. If you're finding your plants aren't thriving, consider what system you've got and whether your crop is suited to that design in the first place. Roots need space and air, too, so the last thing you want is constant immersion. Check that your roots aren't too deep into your nutrient water and rotting.

14.4 N is for Nutrients

An aquaponics system uses nutrients dissolved in water for plants to take up directly. It's a common misconception that an aquaponics arrangement will provide all nutrient needs for all plants simply because of the fish waste. Fish waste is dependent on fish food, which is designed solely for fish needs without leaving excess nutrients that plants need. Many nutrient levels are deficient in aquaponics because growers don't take this into account. Potassium deficiency is especially prevalent.

Adding nutrients is a delicate science. You risk changing pH and other levels in your system by adding the nutrients to the water. Similarly, some additives are not organic. If you plan on selling your product, you'll have to be aware of what you can and can't add to fix deficiencies. Many deficiencies have similar symptoms, so it can be a guessing game which one your plants have. Iron, Calcium, and Potassium are the most commonly needed additives, but they also affect pH and require careful monitoring.

14.5 S is for Support

Most aquaponics designs require adapting to your available space. Plants and tanks need to be properly supported for everything to grow and be maintained. Having tanks at an accessible-height is a good start because it will make them easier to maintain and to cater to the needs of your plants. Taller plants need support, and many heavier fruits will also need support to stop the crops from getting wet or mildewed from being too close to the nutrient solution. System design goes a long way when it comes to being successful.

So that's the basics of Meg Stout's SWANS. Is that everything to make your infallible system? Far from it. Let's add another acronym for the things it's missing – POLISH.

- Problems

- Observation

- Learning

- Interaction

- Supplies

- Help

Problems

How can problems make you successful? That seems truly counterproductive! Problems are learning experiences, and this is especially true for aquaponics. If you don't experience the problems like pests, nutrient deficiencies, and such, then how will you handle them when they do crop up (and they will).

Pest control is often overlooked in aquaponics because people wrongly assume that indoor plants are not susceptible. We've seen that blue light can be used as a form of pest control. Still, because of your fish, you'll want to avoid the traditional pesticides and insecticides which can kill your fish and also affect your crop quality. To be successful, your plants need to be free of predators, and the best way to do this is through observation.

If you're paying enough attention to your system, you'll not only notice nutrient issues and small adjustments for pH, temp, etc. but you'll be able to spot predators before they become a real problem. Cabbage worms, for example, are a real headache, and when not spotted early enough, can absolutely ravage a crop.

Plant debris is the ideal media for flies and pests to multiply. Sick plants have organic debris that's often literally decomposing on the plant, and this attracts pests. Keeping your plants healthy is one of the most efficient ways to ward off pests. You can also use other non-harmful insects to naturally prey on the ones which are pests. Check out the project where scientists used ladybirds to eat aphids and save crops without pesticides. This is ideal for greenhouse conditions. You can monitor the beneficial insects and keep them in the area for maximum effect.

Observation

It can't be said enough that you need to pay attention to your system. Without observation, it's easy to suddenly find you've got a major problem that could potentially mean either an entire redesign or cycling the system and losing everything. Observation means not only keeping everything running smoothly, but it means avoiding predators, deficiencies, and keeping track of everything – even when your system is running perfectly smoothly.

Having logs is part of running an aquaponics system because it allows you to go back to the last thing changed and to predict when anything may potentially become a problem. Observation will help make your system infallible by giving you the ability to predict problems through familiarity. It's part of the learning process that you need to get so familiar with your system that it will seem like you don't get problems anymore because you can head them off early.

Learning

Learning is actually part of the observation. As you observe your system, you'll begin to learn its nuances and predict its needs. Learning is also part of reaching out to others to learn new techniques and new ways of handling common problems.

While at this point, you may feel that you've got everything down, technology is constantly advancing, and simply relying on automation isn't learning. Complacency with your system through automation is a great way to lose your crops.

Most classes you're going to come across are intended for colleges or beginners. For those intermediate students who are already familiar with how aquaponics works, the best way of learning is to reach out and familiarize yourself with others in the community. In your infallible system, learning is just one of the tools to get you there. If you don't learn, you'll make the same mistakes over and waste time and money.

Learning also means having knowledge. Knowledge about pest control, the signs of deficiencies, etc. A knowledgeable grower is a successful grower.

Interaction

I know that automation has its appeal, especially if you're starting small and don't have much help. It can seem a daunting task to monitor nitrogen levels, plant roots, nutrient levels, fish health, and that's without getting into the minute details of light wavelengths. Interaction with your system means taking it a step further than simple observation, and you have to have both. It's no good simply observing your system and noting the issues; you have to experiment and fix them.

Similarly, you'll want to have interaction with others so that you can expand your knowledge base and tackle problems as they arise. Interacting with others often offers a fresh perspective on issues. While you may still not find a solution, your system will be much less likely to fail thanks to the improved knowledge.

Supplies

If you want to be successful, you'll need quality equipment. Having the right equipment isn't cheap, and it's that initial investment that puts many people off. Buying from a reputable supplier means you're not getting contaminants that might come from second-hand drums. Similarly, getting good quality seeds and plants will make a difference in how well they grow. Quality seeds come from reputable growers, and since your system is delicate, you must stick with organics. Some seed growers will coat their seeds in fertilizers to grow better, which, being designs for soil, means they may harm your fish is put into an aquaponic bed.

Successful aquaponics plants start as a quality seed. You can't expect to grow great plants from poor seeds. Choose heirloom varieties where possible. It's often impossible to get growers guarantees when you're trying to start them in your system, but remember too, you can't swap seedlings from soil to aquaculture, which means if you don't want to start your own seeds, you'll need to find seed plugs that have already been started in an aquaponic system.

While this might seem more appropriate for the SWANS portion, the reason, its part of POLISH is because you always need to be thinking one crop ahead, especially if you're doing this for commercial profit. Having the next crop planned and sold before even planting is the ideal way to get head and ensure your success.

Help

As with learning, you'll often find you don't have the answers. In fact, since aquaponics is still a relatively new field, you may still find that no one has the answers.

When you ask for help, you're not coming across as stupid but willing to learn from those who have more experience. It's one of the toughest things for anyone who has passed the beginner stage to master because it's humbling. We're often the most knowledgeable of our group, and not having the answers can be tough to swallow.

The best place to get help is from your peers; there's a huge chance they've had the same problem before, or someone has had something similar. Failure is another key to success here as you'll likely learn more from your failures than your successes.

So while SWANS will get your system running, it's unlikely to get it thriving, which is why you need POLISH. POLISH gets you familiar with your system and tackling the issues that might arise from it.

Conclusion

Aquaponic gardening is a great way to grow fruit and vegetables in a small area. It is a very sustainable and environmentally friendly method of growing food.

If you live in an area where water is scarce, expensive, or the soil is of poor quality, aquaponics makes for a very easy way to have a thriving vegetable garden. It requires very little work once it is filled and has no reliance on the soil at all.

The big advantage of aquaponics is that you can plant at a much higher density than in soil because there is no competition between the plants for resources. You can usually plant up to ten times more plants within an aquaponic garden than you can in the same area of soil. This means that aquaponic systems are incredibly productive and will produce massive amounts of food for you. It is far more efficient to grow aquaponically rather than growing in soil.

Because you are dealing with soil, weeds are really not a problem with an aquaponic garden. They really are very low-maintenance once they are set up and just require a quick daily check to ensure everything is ok. Pests tend to be less of a problem as well because you are growing them in water.

With grow lamps, you can extend your growing season or even grow fresh vegetables all year round. If you live in an area with a short growing season, this is a big benefit because you can grow plants that require a longer growing season in areas where they wouldn't grow naturally.

Aquaponic gardening is a very environmentally friendly way for you to grow vegetables. It is pretty easy for you to set up your own system at home. You can either make one yourself, or you can buy one of the many pre-made systems and assemble it at home. You can make your system as big as you want it to grow as much food as you want to.

It isn't difficult to get started with this form of gardening, and it's very fun and enjoyable. As a side benefit, you can keep fish in the tank that you can eat! You can keep carp, trout, and many other types of fish, as long as they aren't salt-water fish. Other people prefer to keep fish that are more decorative. You can even keep tropical fish in your aquaponic system if you heat the water.

Just remember not to overpopulate your tank with too many fish, particularly to start with, because it can make the fish ill and stop them from growing. If you plan on eating your fish, you need to make sure there is room for them to grow in the tank, to a size where they are ready for eating.

There is a lot you can do with an aquaponic system. You can be as adventurous as you want in your design and setup or make it as simple as you want. It can become a crowning feature in your house, or set up as a food production plant in your garage.

Remember that plants grow in an aquaponic system is usually half the time it would take in soil. Lettuce could take at least sixty days to mature in soil but will take just under thirty days to mature in a hydroponic system.

This is one of the best ways to grow food in an organic and environmentally friendly way. With water becoming more scarce and expensive, and many areas of the world having poor soil quality, aquaponic gardening is becoming a much more viable way of growing food.

Its fun to grow fish and vegetables this way at home, and you will love the yield and the taste of them. Now you have the know-how to set up your own aquaponic system and start growing your own food at home using this fascinating method.